SYMBOLS

SOIL
REQUIREMENTS

Light,
sandy soil

Humus,
treated soil

LIGHT
REQUIREMENTS

Common
garden soil

Sunny

Shady

PLANT
CHARACTERS

Half-shady

Plant decorative
only during
growing period

Evergreen
leaves

MOISTURE
REQUIREMENTS

Plant decorative
until early spring

Drought-
resistant

High moisture
requirements

Normal
moisture
requirements

LAWNS AND
ORNAMENTAL GRASSES

LAWNS AND
ORNAMENTAL GRASSES

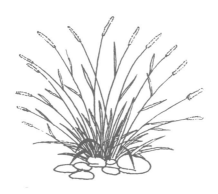

Text by Jan Ondřej and Milada Opatrná

Illustrations by Petr Rob

LAWNS AND ORNAMENTAL GRASSES
Original title Trávníky a okrasné trávy

Copyright © 1997 by Brio, spol. s r.o., Praha
© 1997 English edition Rebo Productions Ltd., London

Text by Jan Ondřej and Milada Opatrná
Illustrated by Petr Rob
Translated by Ivana Kadlecová
Graphic layout and typesetting by Alfa
Colour separation by Repro plus, s.r.o.

ISBN 1 901094 56 1

Printed in Czech Republic.

CONTENTS

What this book is about

This is a book on lawns and ornamental grasses. All lawns form an indispensable part of every garden or park, from those closely and regularly mown to meadow-like types with tall grasses that are mown only occasionally. They play an important aesthetic role. A well-established and well-maintained lawn has a function similar to that of a carpet in your sitting room: it integrates and links all other features.

Together with areas of water, lawns form the lightest parts of a garden: they do not cast any shadows. They adapt easily to the irregularities of the terrain, while at the same time softening its sharp outlines.

A high-quality, well-maintained lawn, harmonious in colour and structure, lends an appearance of tidiness, cleanness and order to a garden or park. It forms a neutral element that unifies all the other features of a garden

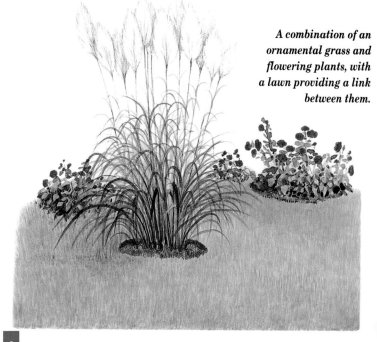

A combination of an ornamental grass and flowering plants, with a lawn providing a link between them.

Ornamental grasses, annual and perennial, and bamboos - these are the symbols of the individual chapters in this book.

or park (trees, shrubs, flowerbeds, walls, pergolas, sculptures and pools). The more compact and the finer its texture (lawns are mostly composed of narrow-leaved grasses), the greater its unifying capacity and the more effective the contrasts, so necessary in garden design.

And what about the individual ornamental grasses? They are mostly grown in the same way as annual or perennial plants, i.e. as solitary specimens or in beds. Most ornamental grass species are interesting complements to other cultivated plants, they soften individual garden compositions and serve as natural links between some contrasting combinations.

The purpose of this book is not to list everything that is known about ornamental grasses and lawns; but rather to provide the reader with detailed instructions on how to care for grasses, together with the necessary background information to enable even amateur gardeners to achieve a fair amount of success in this field.

The importance of lawns and grasses in the garden

If you search for a definition of "lawn" in specialised gardening literature, you will find something like the following: "A lawn is usually an artificial community of plants entirely covering the soil, consisting predominantly of a few prevailing grass species producing small amounts of green matter but many offshoots, having a dense root system that spreads through the vegetation layer of the earth and forms a dense, compact and resilient carpet. Regular mowing and other cultivation methods serve to maintain an appropriate appearance and a fit condition to fulfil all its aesthetic, recreational, and other functions."

The above definition lists the essential properties of a lawn, but what are its functions? Basically, these are of two types: the hidden ones, invisible to us, and the obvious ones, those we recognise immediately.

Hidden functions include the lowering of environmental noise levels, reducing the amount of dust particles in the air (on condition the lawn is not dry, of course), removing noxious gases from the air, and raising air humidity by evaporation through the leaves, which

A bunch of flowering plants may be ablaze with colour, or its tones may be sober. A bouquet of grass inflorescences is always more sober in colour, and it looks more airy.

A lawn in the garden should form a neutral zone that serves as a backdrop to all the other features that together make up the garden.

in addition regulates microclimatic thermal conditions and the circulation of oxygen in the air. It is said that a lawn with a surface area of 100 sq. m produces, in the course of one year, as much oxygen as 10 people use up during that same period of time.

Obvious functions, the ones that can be seen and understood at first sight; include the lawn's contribution to the aesthetic effect of a garden - lawns form the basic element of most garden designs.

Lawns are also suitable for all kinds of sports and other recreational activities, they capture precipitation (if a lawn is well-established, puddles never form on it, not even after heavy showers). On sloping terrain, lawns prevent large-scale water erosion.

Most of the above-mentioned functions can be performed only by well-conditioned, healthy lawns. Foremost among its functions is the aesthetic one, as it exerts a positive influence on the human mind and soul.

Types of lawn

Lawns are usually established as a long-lasting culture. To make it as long-lasting as possible, the species of grass used should be suitable for the soil, climate and other characteristics of the given site. For even a very small stretch of lawn to have an appropriate effect, it should consist of grass species of similar growth and with leaves of similar shape, width and colour.

Whether or not to allow the growth of broad-leaved plants (i.e. dicotyledons), usually referred to as lawn weeds (such as dandelion, daisy, ground elder, creeping buttercup), on the lawn, will depend mainly on the type of lawn we want to have. A fine, strictly ornamental lawn, with a marked aesthetic function, should not contain any admixtures of broad-leaved plants. The maintenance of such a lawn, however, is extremely demanding. In

lawns used for recreational activities such as sports and sunbathing - which will have to cope with a certain amount of trampling - a greater variety of species can be allowed. By contrast, if you want to create a flower meadow,

A garden lawn should be kept short, so that it allows easy movement on its surface.

dicotyledonous species with bright flowers are indispensable. Depending on its desired appearance, and its maintenance characteristics, each lawn belongs to either of two basic groups: intensive or extensive lawns.

Intensive lawns

These are mown several times a year, depending on their function and purpose, usually often to very often (6-20 times). Furthermore, an ample amount of fertiliser is applied regularly, they are watered according to need (or possibility), and they are weeded and otherwise maintained in the best possible shape. This group includes the ornamental and recreational lawns mentioned above.

Extensive lawns

These need only minimal care, they are mown just once, twice, or at most three times a year, and are given only just enough nutrients to avoid their becoming too thin or being infested with weeds. Lawns belonging to this group should form a rich root system and not much growth above the ground. They include flower meadows.

Portable garden accessories facilitate lawn maintenance.

Use of ornamental grasses in the garden

Thanks to their growth, coloration and in some species even their inflorescences, ornamental grasses are a specific, striking and irreplaceable feature of every garden and park.

They are better suited to gardens of a free, irregular, seemingly natural design than to those arranged strictly geometrically. They look well planted along the margins of pools and lakes, and can also be used as bed borders or as a background for some garden corners.

Certain low-growing species can be used for creating uniform and unicoloured ground covers under trees and they are also a good choice for xerophilous (drought-loving) arrangements in roof gardens (particularly when these are placed on roofs of moderate strength not able to support more than a thin layer of soil).

Infructescences of various reed species; these do not belong to the grass family, but are very similar in appearance and may be used as an attractive indoor winter decoration.

With few exceptions, ornamental grasses are not grown for the beauty of their inflorescences. They can serve as a dominant feature in beds of gaily flowering annuals, or, on the contrary, as a neutral unifying element or as a complement to other plants, to underline and harmonise the final effect. In other words: grasses are used in flower beds in the same way as sprigs of asparagus fern complement bunches of cut flowers. The aesthetic effect of grasses is not dependent on their time of flowering, but lasts practically throughout their entire growing season.

Spikes, spikelets, panicles, pseudospikes - these are all botanical names of grass inflorescences. The difference with those of other ornamental plants - roses, sunflowers, poppies or dahlias - is obvious. This is due to the evolution of grasses on our planet.

Grasses belong to the large family of wind-pollinated plants. In these plants, the transfer of pollen from anthers to stigmas, necessary for reproduction, is carried out by the wind. Wind-pollinated plants differ markedly from the gaily coloured insect-pollinated plants, where this task is performed by insects (mostly bees). The rich coloration of the flowers serves to attract the pollinators.

A bunch of dry grass panicles creates an airy effect and makes a long-lasting winter decoration in a vase.

Criteria of choice of ornamental grasses

Grasses come mostly in various shades of green, but some have yellow or silver-striped leaves, while greyish blue or bluish green varieties also exist. In autumn, many grasses attain more vivid, warmer colour shades - brownish, yellowish or even orange. A number of grass species have dry tufts offering visual pleasure even in the winter months. Snow-covered beds with yellow or brown fluttering leaves dusted with snow or decorated with hoarfrost and rustling pleasantly at the slightest breeze may become a source of pleasure for every sensitive person.

In addition to a variety of colours, ornamental grasses also offer a wide range of sizes to choose from - from blue fescue (*Festuca glauca*), up to 15 cm high, up to *Miscanthus floridulus*, which attains a height of 3 m. Grasses also differ in their habit - from the rigidly tufted, erect members of the

It is a good idea to separate the lawn from a flowering wall or a rockery by a paved path or crazy paving.

Miscanthus genus via the clump-forming species blue oat grass (*Helictotrichon sempervirens*), pampas grass (*Cortaderia selloana*) or cord grass (*Spartina michauxiana*) with arched leaves to the runner-forming species that spread widely, such as false oat grass (*Arrhenatherum elatius* var. *bulbosum* 'Variegatum') or sea lyme grass (*Elymus arenarius*).

As to bamboos, even these differ in the height they attain. Many bamboo species grow quite well in the Mediterranean, but in the colder parts of Europe, the frost-resistance of the individual species must be considered. The choice is therefore, naturally, rather limited.

Some grass species (e.g. *Briza media* or *Calamagrostis* x *acutiflora*) combine well with heath plants, others are suited to hot and dry places and sun-facing parts of a rockery (e.g. blue fescue, *Festuca glauca* or reed meadow grass, *Glyceria maxima*). Ornamental grasses can also be combined with plants of a similar habit and leaf shape, for instance with yuccas (*Yucca filamentosa*) or sweet flag (*Acorus calamus*).

A grass-covered path. Remember that sandy or paved paths are not the only solution for connecting individual parts of a garden.

Before laying a lawn

Garden and park lawns are usually established as long-lasting growths that are to last for several decades. This has led specialists from countries with a long tradition in lawn-making to come up with the following rule: prepare the site with care and wait a while before you sow. Success in establishing a high-quality long-lasting lawn can be said to be depend for up to 75 per cent on meticulous and careful preparation of the soil. This is where we have to look for the cause of any differences in the quality of similar lawns from various owners or rather various gardeners.

Before you start laying a lawn, you should make up your mind about what you expect of it, as this determines your next steps. As you gain some experience with lawns, you will come to realise not all lawns are the same.

In places where cars are to be parked more or less regularly, it is a good idea to lay two compact rows of paving slabs with a stretch of lawn in between, with or without stepping stones.

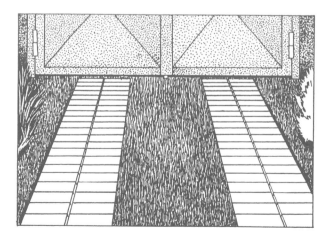

A good solution for paths in a lawn are prefabricated concrete slabs used as stepping stones or crazy paving laid on the level of the original lawn surface.

Laying a lawn, step by step

1) Consider carefully what functions your new lawn is to have and what type you want to go for;
2) choose the right site for it;
3) have the soil tested;
4) construct a watering or drainage system, if necessary;
5) level the terrain;
6) prepare the layer of top soil;
7) let the soil settle down;
8) choose the right seed;
9) sow the seed;
10) take care of the newly grown lawn.

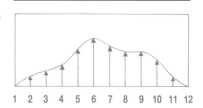

The diagram shows varying grass growth activity during the year. Grass growth peaks around June, with a secondary peak in September. During these peak periods, the lawn has the highest need for nutrients, water and other care.

Types of lawn

Apart from the aesthetic aspects of lawns, which have already been mentioned (their size, colour, structure and linking function), individual lawns mainly differ in their specific use in a garden or a park, i.e. in how they meet our needs.

This is easy to see. An ornamental lawn will require a different choice of species than a lawn used for sports; the mix of species suitable for a meadow is different again, and lawns will also greatly differ according to local conditions: sunny or damp and shady. The limited scope of this book leaves no space for more detailed information on for instance the specific requirements of golf greens and football grounds.

The untrained eyes of a layman visiting a park or garden will not spot a great deal of difference in the composition of grassy areas, even though their functions are quite obvious. We tend to apply the word "lawn" even to stretches of land covered with a self-sown community of plants generally known as weeds, only a negligible part of which are true grasses. The reason for this is that grasses, unlike trees and shrubs, are tiny, inconspicuous plants. They are thus not perceived as individuals, but as a whole; furthermore, the individual grass species are often so similar that you need a magnifying glass to distinguish them properly.

Types of grass used for lawns

According to their habit and their method of spreading, lawn grasses fall

Perennial grasses can be easily propagated by the division of clumps, which is usually done with a spade.

into three basic groups: tuft-forming grasses grow from one place, their tufts only increasing in size; grasses which spread by surface runners, with new plants forming and taking root at the ends of the runners (the same system is used by some strawberries); and finally the species sending out rhizomes (creeping stems growing below the surface) that produce daughter plants.

The method of spreading has a direct influence on the density of the turf. If you want to have dense, long-lasting lawns, runner-forming species (*Poa pratensis, Agrostis tenuis*) must prevail in the composition over the tuft-forming ones (*Lolium perenne, Festuca ovina*). This is particularly a must when lawns have to be resistant to much tramping of feet (such as sports grounds and children's playgrounds). The tuft-forming species make up the framework, with the runner-forming species spreading among them. Together they produce the necessary firm structure of a permanent lawn.

Put the detached part of the tuft into a sufficiently large hole, press soil towards the roots and water properly.

Grass with surface runners

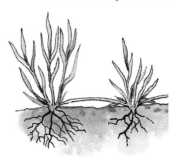

Tuft-forming grass

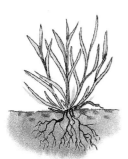

Grass with rhizomes (creeping stems growing below the surface)

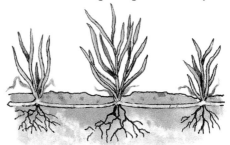

Care of the lawn

As every other piece of work created by man, each lawn needs a certain amount of work to keep it in a state that is adequate to meet our requirements, and to perform its function.

As we are talking of a community of living plants, the word care is more appropriate than maintenance. The more demanding you are as to the lawn's appearance, and the more intense the use it is put to, the more work it will need to keep it in a good state. The amount of time and money you want to spend on your lawn is thus entirely up to you. The perfect grassy carpet does not come into being spontaneously - on the contrary, it will be the result of many years of hard, demanding and patient work. Of course, if your daily business leaves you little spare time of if you are simply not prepared to spend your precious leisure time on this kind of work, nothing terrible will happen, but the state of your lawn will reflect this. The best solution in this case may be to leave the care of your lawn to a professional - many gardening firms specialise in lawns and their services are widely advertised.

Lawn care involves more than just mowing. When mowing, you trim the leaves and stems, and the clippings then have to be gathered and put on the compost heap. Too frequent mowing results in depleting the soil of nutrients, which must be supplied by regular feeding. If you want to have your lawn to be free of dicotyledonous plants (i.e. weeds), you will have to remove these by a method of your choosing. Sometimes (particularly in early spring) lawns welcome some rolling down, frequently cut and heavily trampled-down lawns profit from vertical loosening and aerating of the soil. Other

If you want to maintain the colour of a tuft of perennial grass, do not let the inflorescences ripen.

Spreading of runner-forming grasses (e.g. in a flowerbed) can be prevented by sinking a prefabricated concrete cylinder or a ring of thick foil into the soil and planting the grass in the middle.

To prevent dicotyledonous plants from infesting the lawn, sink a wide band of foil in the soil between lawn and bed.

methods of care include trimming the edges of a lawn, where it borders on garden beds and paths, mending damaged patches, filling in hollows etc., but sometimes you even have to combat diseases or pests.

This short survey suffices to show that a good lawn entails continuously repeated work. Without this, natural processes will eventually turn the lawn into a community of plants with completely different features from those you originally had in mind for your stretch of land.

Basic lawn types

As mentioned earlier, lawns are divided according to their functions into ornamental, recreational and flowering ones. When we consider the term "ornamental", we can conclude that even a football ground has its aesthetic value, the same as a meadow full of flowering plants. However, a football ground is not an ornamental lawn, its ornamental value is only a secondary feature. It has been created for other purposes - to provide the best possible terrain for this sport. An ornamental lawn has a different function - it should always be established and maintained just for aesthetic reasons.

Ornamental lawns

Such types of lawns are established with one single aim - to please the eye. They are not intended for sunbathing, for playing ball games or for any other recreational activities. Their only role in gardens and parks is an aesthetic one - they are in fact works of art. For this specific aim, they require a special choice of grass species and intensive care.

Choice of grasses

As far as grass species are concerned, you should always choose species and varieties capable of forming a fine lawn, well-balanced in colour. These are mostly specially cultivated varieties, with leaves that are less than 0.5 cm wide, of the following species: browntop (*Agrostis tenuis*), red fescue (*Festuca rubra*), sheep's fescue (*F. ovina*) and smooth-stalked meadow grass (*Poa pratensis*). The first two species mentioned will not tolerate heavy traffic.

Grass mixtures for various lawn colour shades

If you can compose your own mixture of pure species and varieties, you can determine the final shade of

A path can also be made of sparsely laid prefabricated square slabs.

your lawn. The basic mixture consists of 40 per cent red fescue (*Festuca rubra*) and the same amount of creeping red fescue (*F. rubra* ssp. *genuina*).

To get a deeper green, add 20 per cent browntop; if you prefer a bluish green shade, replace this with the same proportion of creeping bent (*Agrostis stolonifera*). A yellowish green shade can be obtained by complementing the basic *Festuca* species with 20 per cent velvet bent (*Agrostis canina*).

The rate of cover, i.e. the quantity of seed per sq. m, is also important. If the soil has been well prepared, and if the seeds are not older than three years, the rate of cover need not be very high. With the mixtures mentioned above, the recommended amount is 12 g of seed per sq. m.

An ornamental lawn should not be walked on without need. This can be avoided by putting in stepping stones where some traffic is expected.

Recreational lawns

This group includes all types of lawn established to tolerate trampling feet and people playing ball games or sunbathing - in short, for recreational activities. This type of lawn is the most common in the vicinity of residential areas.

In addition to proper preparation of the soil, the choice of suitable grass species is also important: the grasses used should show some resistance to the trampling of feet. If the traffic on such a lawn is spread regularly over the entire surface, the damage is never so great as when it is limited to certain spots. If activity takes place on only some parts of the lawn, the soil there gradually gets compacted, the grass roots are deprived of oxygen, growth is stunted and finally individual plants die off altogether. The result is a bare, compacted patch of soil that absorbs hardly any water. The soft tissues of new growth also suffer from much trampling.

Like ornamental lawns, recreational lawns also belong to the intensive types.

Choice of species

The basic grasses for lawns that are to resist heavy trampling are perennial ryegrass (*Lolium perenne*) and smooth-stalked meadow grass (*Poa pratensis*), with lesser timothy (*Phleum nodosum*) and crested dog's tail (*Cynosurus cristatus*) to complement them.

In heavy soils and in places with a compact soil surface, *Lolium perenne* has a more permanent growth and longer life than in light, sandy, loose soils that dry out easily. However, it does not tolerate permanently wet soils or lengthy dry spells. *Poa pratensis* should constitute about 20-40 per cent of mixtures for lawns that are to resist heavy trampling. This is the most permanent of all grass species, even though it develops very slowly after germination (taking 3-4 years to reach full size). It forms a firm, compact turf and grows in quickly after having been cut. As it forms a great number of underground stems, it is suitable for filling in bare patches caused by much

traffic. It is highly resistant to trampling and will grow well in any locality.

Care

The need for appropriate care increases with the intensity of the trampling the lawns are subjected to. To maintain the lawn in good condition, regular feeding is important. You should also carry out all that is necessary for the turf to become denser, particularly vertical scarifying and aerating the soil down to a depth of about 8 cm (to repair the compacting caused by trampling). In the hot and dry summer months, the lawn benefits from watering. It is advisable to water infrequently but in large amounts, so that the layer of top soil gets sufficiently moist.

Dried-out lawns cannot serve their purpose properly and suffer more from trampling.

A dog can damage your lawn by trampling down paths in it (particularly large, heavy breeds), by digging in it or by defecating and urinating on it.

Flower meadows

Maintaining ornamental and recreational lawns in proper condition is quite time-consuming and demands a lot of effort. No wonder then that in the seventies, there was a tendency in a number of countries towards more ecologically balanced grass communities including dicotyledonous plants as well as grasses. These communities needed hardly any interference throughout the growing season.

Whether to go for a lawn requiring intensive care or for a flower meadow is a decision that no specialist can make for you. It will depend on your own conditions and demands.

Below we list some of the advantages and disadvantages of flower meadows.

Advantages

An ecologically balanced meadow community, rich in species, usually is

You can create a flower meadow by planting various perennials and bulbs in a stretch of lawn.

A meadow with flowering dicotyledonous plants

ablaze with colour from May till October; it need not (and should not) be fertilised, but some watering is welcome during the growing season. It should be mown two or three times a year at the most (one mowing in June and another one in September will usually do). Such a flower meadow forms an important living environment for a number for small living creatures.

Disadvantages

A flower meadow is aesthetically pleasing only when it is in flower, i.e. approximately from May till the end of September. It does not tolerate any trampling and therefore cannot be used for recreational activities (sunbathing, ball games etc.), which devastate them; traces caused by walking on an unmown flower meadow remain visible for a very long time.

Of course you don't have to turn your whole garden into a flower meadow. Usually it will do to choose just a small stretch of lawn in some distant corner of your garden and change it into a kind of "meadow reserve", or to transform a flowerbed into a "flower meadow". Some gardening firms have seen this marketing niche, and sell packets of mixed seed for establishing miniature flower meadows only a few square metres in size.

Basic grass species for lawns

In principle, three different individual mixtures would do for the three lawn types already mentioned: ornamental lawn, utility or recreational lawn, and flower meadow. The mixtures, however, may also differ according to the locality of the lawn - mixtures exist for dry, hot sites, and for damp, lightly shaded places. These two will usually do for amateur gardening.

The best grass mixtures are those custom-made for your garden by specialised firms. Less frequently such mixtures are prepared by the gardener himself from the individual species and varieties according to a special recipe. This method is rather more demanding, and furthermore it depends on the availability of the individual species on the market. On the other hand, it does make some sense. Every single site where we want to establish a lawn has its own specific features that suit some grass species better than others. To

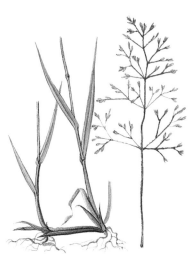

Browntop, Agrostis tenuis, *is a runner-forming species best suitable for ornamental lawns.*

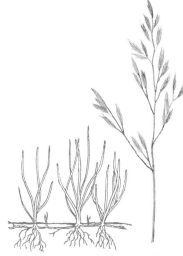

Creeping red fescue, Festuca rubra, ssp. genuina *is a runner-forming species in very wide use.*

illustrate this point, we give some sample recipes for various lawn mixtures:

A mixture for an ornamental lawn in dry situations: 40 per cent *Poa pratensis*, 20 per cent *Festuca rubra* ssp. *fallax*, 20 per cent *Festuca rubra* ssp. *genuina*, 20 per cent *Festuca ovina*.

A mixture for an intensively cultivated shaded lawn: 30 per cent *Festuca rubra* ssp. *genuina*, 20 per cent *Festuca rubra* ssp. *fallax*, 25 per cent *Festuca ovina*, 20 per cent *Poa pratensis*, 5 per cent *Agrostis tenuis*.

A mixture for a recreational lawn: 40 per cent *Poa pratensis*, 25 per cent *Festuca rubra* ssp. *genuina*, 20 per cent *Lolium perenne*, 10 per cent *Cynosurus cristatus*, 5 per cent *Phleum nodosum*.

If you want to convert the percentages into weight units, decide first on the quantity of seed required (e.g. 30,000 seeds per sq. m), using the table on page 31, which lists the number of seeds per gram for each species.

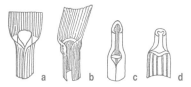

The membranous ligules in the leaf sheaths are probably the best distinguishing feature at the time when grasses are not in flower.
a) **Agrostis tenuis,** *b)* **Festuca rubra ssp. genuina,** *c)* **Festuca rubra ssp. fallax,** *d)* **Festuca ovina.**

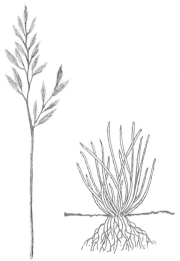

Chewing fescue, **Festuca rubra,** *ssp.* **fallax** *is a tuft-forming species suitable for many types of lawn.*

Sheep's fescue, **Festuca ovina,** *is a tuft-forming species that tolerates drought and full sun best of all grass species.*

Composition of ready-made lawn mixtures

If you decide to buy one of the ready-made mixtures, you should know the following basic facts.

The popular mixtures usually include some of the 15 grass species most commonly used (most of them, however, in several varieties). These 15 species are listed in the table on the opposite page together with information on their use. You should not take this information as dogma, however. Most grass species are noted for a high degree of adaptability to different habitats.

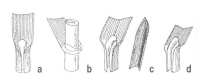

The membranous ligules in the leaf sheaths are probably the best distinguishing feature at the time when grasses are not in flower.
a) Cynosurus cristatus,
b) Lolium perenne, c) Poa pratensis,
d) Poa nemoralis.

Perennial ryegrass, Lolium perenne, is the basic tuft-forming component of lawns for sports as it is very tolerant of being trampled down.

Crested dog's tail, Cynosurus cristatus, is a tuft-formig species for more damp conditions.

Grass species	Suitable for						
	ornamental lawns	utility lawns	flower meadows	tolerant of shade	tolerant of drought	water requirements	number of seeds per gram
Phleum nodosum	–	+	–	–	–	–	2000
Phleum pratense	–	–	+	–	–	+	2000
Lolium perenne	–	+	+	+	+	–	500
F. rubra ssp. fallax	+	–	+	+	+	–	1000
F. rubra ssp. genuina	+	+	+	+	+	–	1000
Festuca pratensis	–	–	+	–	–	–	800
Festuca ovina	+	–	–	–	+	–	2000
Poa nemoralis	–	–	+	+	–	+	5500
Poa pratensis	+	+	+	+	+	–	5000
Deschampsia caespitosa	+	+	–	+	+	–	4000
Cynosurus cristatus	–	+	+	–	–	+	1710
Alopecurus pratensis	–	–	+	–	–	–	1100
Agrostis tenuis	+	–	–	–	–	+	15000
Agrostis stolonifera	–	–	+	–	–	+	10000
Dactylis glomerata	–	–	+	–	–	–	550

Smooth-stalked meadow grass, Poa pratensis, is the basic species for both utility and ornamental lawns.

Wood meadow grass, Poa nemoralis, is suited to lightly shaded situations; it does not like frequent mowing.

Basic grass groups

The individual grass groups can best be distinguished at the time of flowering. However, they are usually not allowed to produce flowers in regularly mown lawns, so some other features have to be used to distinguish between them.

According to their habit, grasses are divided into two basic groups: tuft-forming and runner-forming types, which are further divided into those with rhizomes and those with surface runners. The method of spreading has a direct influence on the density of the turf. If you want your lawn to be dense and long-lived, then the runner-forming species should prevail over the tuft-forming ones. This is particularly important for utility lawns used for sports activities.

Ready-made, commercial lawn mixtures should never be of unknown composition; the box or packet should

Cocksfoot, Dactylis glomerata, *is the basic tuft-forming species for meadow-like lawns; it tolerates shading quite well.*

Timothy, Phleum pratense, *grows best in rather heavy soils. For much-frequented utility lawns, the low-growing lesser timothy is more commonly used.*

Tufted hair-grass, **Deschampsia caespitosa,** *is a dense tuft-forming species, easily adaptable to the most varied conditions.*

give exact information on the species it contains, the percentage of each species, and also the type of lawn the mixture is intended for. The buyer can thus easily choose the right mixture for the conditions of his or her lawn. Equally important is it for the packet to mention the year of harvesting (four-year-old seed is almost worthless), and also how many square metres can be sown with the amount in the packet (about 1-2 kg of mixture should be sufficient for 100 sq. m of lawn). The packet should also give detailed sowing instructions.

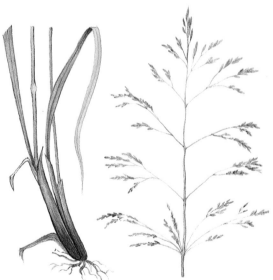

Golden foxtail, **Alopecurus pratensis,** *is a clump-forming species suitable for meadows, and it does best in damp, inundated, rather heavy soils.*

Preparing the ground for a lawn

It is a tried and tested truth that careful and thorough preparation of the soil for the future lawn before sowing takes you almost three quarters of the road towards success. After the seeds have been sown and the lawn starts to grow in, you will hardly be able, or willing, to improve the soil conditions, to change its structure, water retention, physical composition etc.

Soil composition

To a lawn, the most important aspect of its growing position is the soil; of course the same goes for all plants,. We should therefore carefully look at the soil before we lay a lawn. Most suitable is so-called semi-heavy soil. If you have a soil test done (which can only be recommended), the best soils consist predominantly (70-80 per cent) of sandy particles measuring about 0.25-2 mm across. Soils in which smaller particles prevail are less favourable for lawns. Heavy, clayey soils can be improved by mixing them with sand. Light, sandy soils, by contrast, are enriched with clayey and humus-rich substrates. It is quite improper to dig in layers of rubble, gravel, plastic materials, scrap metal, wood chips or other similar things in the deeper soil layers, which gardeners sometimes do in the belief that they thus provide the necessary drainage layer. The truth is that you may thus get large or smaller islets of soil with differing physical qualities, e.g. with higher drainage capacity where water is absorbed more rapidly and consequently the lawn dries out more quickly. Also, when organic materials decompose, they shrink, and the lawn will develop hollows.

Air and humus content, soil acidity

Soil for lawns should be airy, porous - air should make up about 10-15 per cent of the soil volume. Air contained in the soil promotes the formation of offshoots and thus improves lawn density.

As for organic particles (humus), ideally they should constitute about 5 per cent of the soil for a lawn.

Equally important for lawns is the soil pH. Most grasses used in lawns do best in slightly acid soils with pH values between 5.5 and 6.5. The more alkaline the soil (pH 7 and higher), the higher the lime content, which favours the growth of dicotyledonous plants (i.e. lawn weeds) to the detriment of grasses.

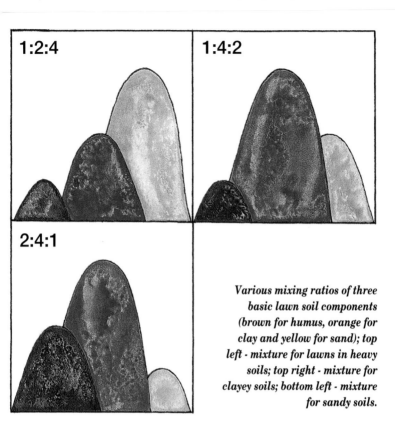

1:2:4

1:4:2

2:4:1

Various mixing ratios of three basic lawn soil components (brown for humus, orange for clay and yellow for sand); top left - mixture for lawns in heavy soils; top right - mixture for clayey soils; bottom left - mixture for sandy soils.

Even if you don't have the soil pH of your lawn tested, you can learn much about its acidity from the occurrence of certain plants (so-called indicators). Alkaline soil is indicated for instance by *Asperula arvensis, Onobrychis viciifolia, Medicago sativa, Sinapis arvensis* or *Tussilago farfara.* Strongly acid soil, in contrast, is revealed e.g. by *Anthemis arvensis* and *Viola tricolor.*

Preparation of the soil

Decisive for lawns is the topmost layer, about 15-20 cm thick, which should be given most attention when digging or ploughing the site for the future lawn. All unsuitable objects (large stones, broken bricks, pieces of wood and tree stumps, and of course also the roots and rhizomes of perennial plants, such as dandelion, ground elder, coltsfoot or thistles) must be removed. The more carefully you work, the easier will be your care of the lawn in the future.

Drainage and watering

The soil and climatic conditions of a future lawn are not always ideal. Sometimes the soil in the plot is too damp - either because of a high underground water table, or because of large quantities of surface water that have flowed on to it. In this case it may be advisable to consider laying some subsurface drainage piping or construct drains filled with gravel.

At some other time the lawn is to be placed in a hot or windy situation. Here you should think of providing a watering system - preferably with an automatic telescopic sprayer.

Drainage system. The pipes are laid in a stony bed with a slight slant towards the main collector. Places where the individual pipes meet are covered with flat stones which prevent fine soil particles from filling the inside of the pipe.

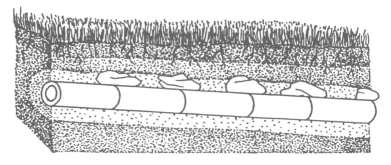

Rough soil particles (i.e. stones larger than 2 cm across) are removed with a garden sieve.

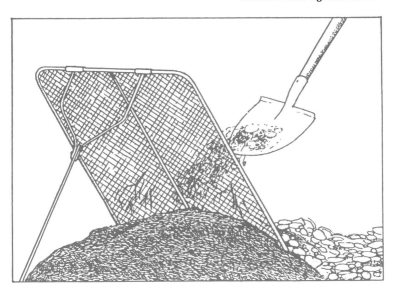

All kinds of building debris - bricks, pieces of concrete, wood offcuts, paper, plastic, broken glass - should be carefully removed.

Soil surface finishing

The final phase of preparing soil for a lawn is the preparation of the surface: harrowing, breaking down the clods, shovelling, raking and rolling. Ultimately, the surface should be smooth, either level or sloping - according to the shape of the terrain - without any marked irregularities, and the surface soil layer should have a granular texture and should be adequately compacted and slightly damp.

And now you might start sowing. If necessary, do so. But skilled lawn makers advise against too much haste. If you manage to prepare the soil in the autumn, it is better to wait until spring with sowing. Soil made ready in spring can be sown in the autumn. The reason for such a delay is not hard to find: if you leave the prepared soil lying bare for a few weeks, the humidity, structure and nutrient condition have time to stabilise. Also, in the meantime, the ubiquitous seeds of many garden weeds will have germinated. Every square metre of the vegetative layer of cultivated soil is said to contain about 50,000 viable seeds (those lying in the topmost 2-cm layer start germinating at once). If you don't start sowing at once, there is a fairly long period of time for these germinating weeds to be removed either mechanically (using a hand-fork, a rake, a hoe, or by slight harrowing), or chemically (spraying with some universal contact weedkiller that is later neutralised in the soil).

If you respect all laws of nature and its developmental cycles, which are usually of a long-term character, you can hardly do any great harm. Such "natural wisdom" can be found in books by authors known for their clear view of life. In Rudyard Kipling's Jungle Book, for instance, it is expressed by the following conceit: "Haste killed the yellow snake who wanted to swallow the Sun". So work carefully when preparing the soil for a future lawn and don't be unnecessarily hasty about the sowing.

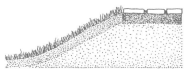

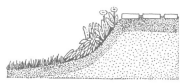

Gentle slopes covered with grass can be easily cut with a mower, while the steep ones are better planted with perennials, low shrubs or plants used as lawn substitutes.

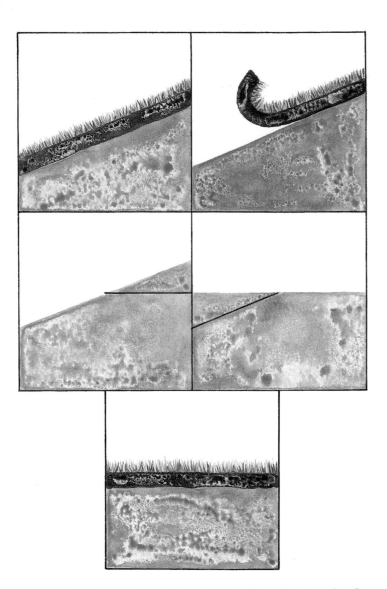

A diagrammatic instruction for levelling a slope to make a lawn (starting from top left towards the bottom): the original grassy slope; careful removing of the turf, if this is of good quality and you want to use it later on when the terrain has been levelled; the top of the slope is dug away and the removed soil is used to fill in the lower part; when the terrain is level, the turf can be laid again.

Methods of laying a lawn

The most common and at the same time the cheapest method of making a lawn is sowing a suitable seex mixture. You can either do it by yourself, following instructions given on the packet, or you can have the work done by a professional gardener.

Time of sowing

There are two generally recommended periods, namely spring, approximately from mid-April till mid-May (this is considered to be the safest time, and is more commonly used), and then at the end of summer, from mid-August till mid-September (sowing at this period can be rather risky). The main reason why these two periods of the year are the best is that there is enough precipitation and that the soil is already (in spring) or still (by late summer) sufficiently warm, which is one of the factors on which germination depends. You can, of course, also sow at any time in between, but you will have to water regularly during the summer. When swollen and ready to germinate, grass seeds are very sensitive to lack of water, and if the topmost soil layer dries out, the seeds perish and you have to sow anew.

Method of sowing

Hand sowing is the commonest and also the cheapest method.

However, it needs some skill and a good assessment of how many seeds you should take in your hand and how many you should release between your fingers while sowing in order to distribute the seeds evenly over the area.

When scattering the seeds by hand, you should also see to it that you don't leave deep footprints behind you.

Short flat boards can easily be fastened to your shoes.

It is therefore a good idea to step on planks that are continuously replaced under your feet as you proceed over the loose surface of the soil. Still better, however, is to fasten two small boards to the soles of your shoes, so that your body weight is distributed over a larger surface area and you don't sink too deeply into the soil.

There are two more things you have to do then. First, you must push the seeds slightly into the layer of top soil with the help of a metal rake, either by knocking its tips against the soil, or by gently raking over the soil surface. The second step is then to firm the soil

lightly, preferably with a roller. If you don't have one, you can again use a wide plank moved continuously along the soil's surface, or you can tamp the soil down using the short boards fastened to your shoes.

The main steps in sowing a lawn (from top left to bottom right): regular sowing of the seeds; pressing the seeds into the soil with a rake about 1 cm deep; firming the soil with a roller weighing about 50 kg; watering (natural or artificial) should be plentiful, but use a fine spray.

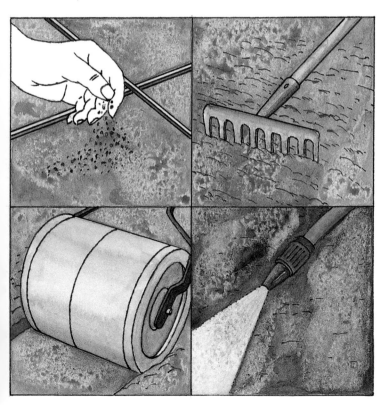

Laying turf

Making a lawn from turf has its indisputable advantages: some bare stretch of land is covered with grass practically in no time (this is particularly important on slopes); you can choose the right type of turf according to its appearance, the function it is to serve, and the conditions of the prepared plot. Also, you don't have to worry about the composition of the lawn mixture, the quantity of seeds, sowing, working the seeds into the soil; and there is less trouble with weeds in pre-grown turf.

If you decide to make your lawn by laying turf, you should keep the following in mind: never lay turf on dry or uncultivated soil; when laying strips or squares of turf, always start laying along the longest side of the plot; rake the soil over slightly before you start laying, so that the grass roots get into

Turf in the form of rolled strips, usually measuring 100x30 cm, is laid on the soil, which has been prepared in the same manner as for sowing.

The strips are laid very close to each other, always in the same direction. Step only on the previously laid turf, not on the prepared bare soil.

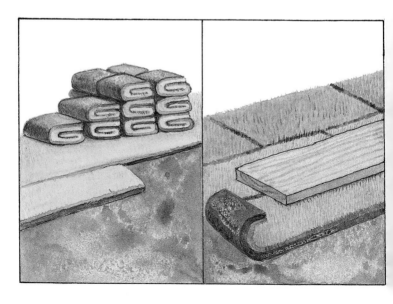

full contact with the soil; while laying the squares or strips, step on the previously laid turf, avoid stepping on the prepared soil; the individual strips must be laid very closely to each other; if covering a slope with turf, start laying at the bottom and continue up to the top; oblong strips should all be laid in the same direction, i.e. either vertically or horizontally.

This work can be done at any time during the growing season, you must, however, always provide sufficient moisture. The turf takes root best at temperatures between 15 and 20 °C, making late summer the best season. Narrow gaps between the squares or strips are filled with fine soil and can be sown with a lawn seed mixture of a composition similar to that used for the turf. The laid turf is slightly firmed with a roller weighing at least 100 kg - all air pockets under the turf are thus removed and turf roots get into closer contact with the soil.

After laying the strips, it is a good idea to fill in the gaps in between with sandy soil, or even sow a few seeds of a similar lawn mixture.

The laid turf is then firmed down with a roller weighing at least 100 kg, and the new lawn must be properly watered to speed up the production of roots.

Lawn maintenance

Each lawn type needs a different kind and amount of care. Intensive lawns are more demanding in this respect, the extensive ones less so. If you want your lawn to fulfil all its functions, you have to maintain and care for it adequately.

"Lawn maintenance" covers several basic jobs that must be carried our either very often or from time to time, but always repeatedly and regularly. The amount and intensity of maintenance work depends on the character of the lawn: the more it is used, and the better and more luxuriant you want it to be, the more care you should give it. On the other hand, the fewer your demands on it, the less work it will need.

Complex lawn maintenance

This is a series of eleven operations following and conditioning one another in a fixed time sequence: mowing, raking and removing the clippings, weeding, fertilising, rolling, watering, trimming the edges, improving the surface, scarification, aerating, combating diseases and pests.

In intensively cultivated lawns, the frequency of these operations varies in the course of the year. The most frequent is mowing and removing of cut grass, then watering (if possible) and fertilising, while all the other activities may be carried out only once or twice a year.

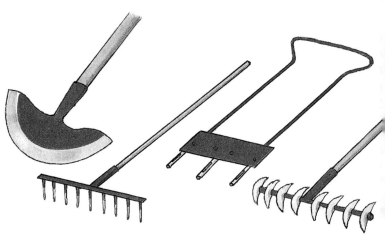

Tools and equipment used in lawn maintenance.

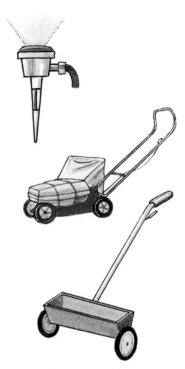

Why well-maintained lawns?

There are several good arguments in favour of well-maintained lawns. For example, they are biologically more active. Frequent mowing causes the grasses to produce new growth and young tissues can transpire and assimilate better. Lawns in which grasses are allowed to flower age more rapidly and tend to dry out, as most of the growing energy is spent on flowering and seed production.

Another important argument for frequent mowing is that it reduces air pollution. Flowering grasses release pollen, which is then carried away by the wind and increases the number of dust particles in the air, which can aggravate allergies. More frequent mowing therefore is important for health reasons as well as because of aesthetics.

The pictures on these two pages show some of the tools and equipment most commonly used for lawn maintenance: a semi-circular edging iron, a rake, an aerator, a special rake for scarifying the turf, a roller, a sprayer, a mower and a mechanical fertiliser distributor.

Mowing

Mowing is the basic operation in lawn maintenance, necessary for all types of lawn. There are, however, big differences in how often they need mowing during the growing season. Flower meadows are mown 1-3 times a year, ornamental, representative and recreational lawns at least 6 times a year, and up to once a week or once a fortnight between April and October.

How often to mow

If you want to have a low grassy carpet in your garden or park, you have to cut it very often - about once a week. Another rule says that you should not cut more than one third to two fifths of the leaves at a time. With the standard height of your lawn at about 4 cm, this means you should mow each time the leaves reach a height of about 5.5-6.5 cm.

A new lawn (produced from seed) must be mown carefully when it reaches a height of about 10 cm. The mower must be very sharp, so that the young grasses are not pulled up with their roots.

How high to mow

Tuft-forming grasses do not tolerate being mown too close; if this is done repeatedly, they will gradually

 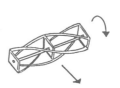 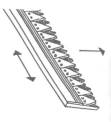

Basic lawn mower systems: the scythe-like system uses a rotating scythe-like blade (left). This is the most widely used system. The spindle-like or knife-like system (centre) is used much less frequently, although it gives the best quality mowing. The grass, however, must not be taller than one-third of the diameter of the spindle. The scissor-like system consists of two sharp-toothed blades that move against each other like scissors. This is particularly suitable for the mowing of extensive lawns.

disappear from the lawn. Runner-forming species, by contrast, do well when mown very close: they become more dense. As both grass types are usually included in lawn mixtures, you cannot entirely satisfy both; you should find a compromise, usually this will be a height of about 3-4 cm. Set your mower to this height.

Mowing equipment

In the past, scythes and sickles were used for this job. These are quite inexpensive and are still much used today, but you need some practice to use them, and working with them may be quite tiring. About a century and a half ago, mechanical mowers were introduced, making lawn mowing much easier, faster and better. They come at a price of course, and for the motorised mowers there is the energy bill to pay.

Lawn mowers fitted with a grass box will save you a lot of raking.

If the blades of your lawn mower are blunt, the grass blades are torn rather than cut (left), and the damaged tissues then dry out and turn yellow. A sharp blade gives a desirable straight cut (right).

There is a wide range of mowers on the market, differing in width, working principle, and type of energy used, among other things.

Choosing a mower

Usually there is a choice of three types of mowing mechanism: scissor-like, knife- or spindle-like, and sickle-like.

As to the type of power, this mostly depends on the local conditions and your personal preference. A mower may be battery- or electricity-driven, it can have a two-stroke or a four-stroke engine, etc.

Maintenance, as well as changing the height of the cut, should be as easy as possible, and the mower should be sturdy, and up to the task.

Removing the clippings

The taller the grass, the easier it is to remove with a rake. The more often you mow, the shorter the clippings and the more difficult they are to remove from the lawn. It is therefore best to

Clippings from lawns mown frequently are very fine, and are difficult to remove from the turf with a rake (only sweeping with a broom will work). If your mower is not fitted with a grass box, a circular scarifying brush may be a good solution. The rotating cylindrical brush placed at the front between the wheels gathers the grass parts and transports them into the container.

collect the clippings into a bag or plastic container mounted on the mower. When using such a collection system, pay attention to the following: the mower should move fast enough or there should be an air stream strong enough to carry the light grass blades to the container; the clippings should be short (longer clippings tend to clog the neck of the container); the grass should be dry (do not use the mower early in the morning or after rain). Special brush-like or vacuum-cleaner-type clippings collectors are also available. The clippings are mostly composted. For those who do so, here is a piece of good advice. The clippings are quite difficult to turn into compost. The thicker the layer of clippings, the longer it takes to turn into compost. If you want to speed up the process, alternate thin layers of clippings with soil or

Diagram of a circular scarifying brush removing clippings.

a mineral substrate. Composting can also be sped up by mixing the clippings with ground limestone.

The clippings can also be used for mulching, e.g. around shrubs or on vegetable beds. This limits evaporation from the soil and also inhibits the growth of weeds.

The rake is the most commonly used tool for the removal of clippings. In the course of time, many different types have been developed, e.g. (left to right): fan-like springy rake with an adjustable spacing of the tines; normal metal or wooden rake (with plastic tines) mostly suitable for hay-making; and a special scarifying rake with sharp blades used for vertical cutting of the lawn and for moss removal.

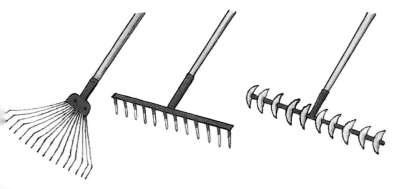

Fertilising

Through frequent mowing, the soil is continuously being depleted of nutrients. The grass continues to grow and uses up all the substances it needs for good growth. It is therefore understandable that the soil must be supplied with new nutrients.

Some people argue that it is better to fertilise less, so that the grass grows more slowly and it is not necessary to mow so often. This, however, is a fallacy. Underfed grasses are weakened and unfit to compete with other plants. Individual grass species differ in the quantity of nutrients they require in the soil. Sheep's fescue, *Festuca ovina*, is among the least demanding, while perennial ryegrass, *Lolium perenne*, is the most demanding grass in this respect. Other species used for lawns are somewhere in between. On an unfertilised lawn, many dicotyledonous plants, particularly deep-rooting ones that can find nutrients in deeper soil layers or those that are able to fix nitrogen from the air (clover), gradually start taking over, and this is exactly what you should avoid.

Several factors influence the character and amount of feeding: the type of lawn and its function, local soil and climatic conditions, the type of weather in the growing season, the humus and nutrient content of the soil, and the amount of money you are willing to spend.

Fertilising by hand needs a lot of practice and great precision, in order to distribute the nutrients evenly over the lawn.

Soil testing

If you want to get objective information on the soil nutrient content of your lawn, the best thing is to have a soil sample tested by a professional on a regular basis. The soil test will tell you which nutrients are lacking from the soil, and what its pH number is, in other words, whether the added nutrients should be acidic or alkaline.

How to fertilise

There are many different fertilising methods. Basically, you can hardly go wrong using a nitrogenous fertiliser sprinkled in April, June and July over the surface of your lawn, 1-2 kg per 100 sq. m, and then about 2 kg of a compound fertiliser (i.e. containing all necessary nutrients) to the same space of lawn. Use the following rule of thumb when feeding: better to use several smaller doses than to feed just once in large amounts.

Applying fertilisers by hand can be as tricky as hand sowing. Each irregularity in amount will soon show up as differently coloured patches in the lawn (dark and light bands). It is therefore better to use a fertiliser spreader or a mechanical distributor for this work.

To guarantee even distribution of the fertiliser, various spreaders can be used in which dosing is controlled by regulating the width of the slot through which the granules are released.

Watering

To grow well and to be sufficiently resistant, grasses need sufficient water. Lawns have been found to need about 400-600 mm of water (either from precipitation or from irrigation) in the period between April and October, evenly distributed in time and space, ideally 2-3 mm a day.

The rule of thumb to use here is: Do not water very often, but abundantly. If there is no rain, then daily short-term watering is not sufficient, as it moistens the soil only to a small depth. Most grasses, however, have their roots at a depth of about 10-20 cm, and water should reach them to be of any use.

Methods of watering

Lawns can be watered in various ways. The simplest methods include surface watering, i.e. hoses fitted with various sprinklers that can be moved from one place to another to gradually cover the whole garden as necessary. You can also use a perforated hose from which water trickles into the surrounding soil. A subsurface trickle irrigation system is rather more complicated and more expensive to construct, but it can reduce water consumption by some 60 per cent compared with surface watering. Another good method is using telescopic sprinklers buried permanently in the soil. When not active, the sprinklers are hidden in their underground cases kept by a spring, so that they are not in the way during lawn

maintenance. When water enters the underground system of pipes and raises the pressure in them, the sprinklers are pushed out of their cases above the surface of the lawn, and they start to rotate, producing circles or arcs of a fine spray. The system can be programmed, and watering can thus be carried out for instance at night for a given period of time.

To conclude, one important note:

A telescopic sprinkler both in action and at rest.

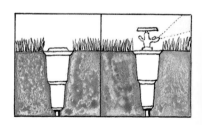

Diagram showing the mounting of the telescopic sprinkler system and the connection to the water mains.

under a tree, the lawn needs twice as much water and nutrients, as the tree roots extract large amounts of both, and the lawn would otherwise suffer.

Various types of transportable sprinklers.

Weeding

It is practically impossible to grow and maintain a lawn entirely free of any dicotyledonous plants (i.e. lawn weeds). Basically, every gardener has just two ways to combat these: by mechanical or chemical means.

Spraying a leaf rosette of a plant with weedkiller.

Mechanical weed control

This consists mostly in the laborious and systematic work of the gardener. The most aggressive weeds should preferably be combated before laying the lawn - by carefully removing all their roots and rhizomes when preparing the soil. Later on you can remove these by digging them out together with their roots, but this is hard work and helps only temporarily. Frequent mowing also limits the growth of weeds.

Chemical weed control

This is the fastest and most effective method, provided that it is carried out with due responsibility with regard to both the choice of the active substance and of application time, and of course also that all the manufacturer's recommendations regarding concentration are respected.

Basically, there are two types of weedkillers to choose from: contact and systemic ones. Contact weedkillers mostly destroy the overground portion of weeds that have come into contact with the active substance, they do not reach the roots. In systemic weedkillers, on the other hand, the active substance is transported from the leaves of an affected weed into the remaining tissues, including the roots, it attacks and destroys the metabolic system, and the plant dies.

The most commonly used contact weedkillers today are GRAMOXONE and REGLONE, the most popular systemic weedkiller is ROUNDUP. One feature they have in common, however, is that they kill all plants they attack, including the grasses. They should therefore be used in the lawn with great care, best by smearing weed leaves carefully with a fine brush. None of the weedkillers mentioned above has any harmful effect on the soil. For large-scale application, however, it is better to use selective weedkillers (i.e. those that attack only broad-leaved weeds) with a systemic effect. Ask at your local garden centre to see what is available. When using some of these preparations, it is advisable to wait with mowing for at least a week after the application.

Moss on the lawn

This usually occurs as a result of too much shade, too much damp, or if the soil is too compact or too acidic (pH below 5.5) or insufficiently fertilised (particularly lacking nitrogen). It can be removed by mechanical means (using a scarifying rake) or chemically (by scattering acid soils with lime or a mixture of three parts sulphate of ammonia and one part blue vitriol in an amount of 5 kg to each 100 sq. m of lawn). Both mechanical and chemical means produce only a transitive effect. For more permanent results, you will have to remove the main cause.

Weeds with regenerating roots or rhizomes should be removed carefully using a trowel.

For the others, you can use a special hand fork.

This fan-like spring-tine rake is used for removing all flower remnants from the lawn after mowing.

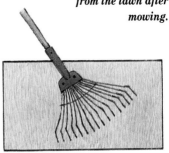

Using a spade to cut away the overground portion of a weed.

Rolling and scarification

These two jobs serve to treat the layer of top soil in a lawn.

Lawn rolling

This operation performed in spring fastens the soil around grass roots, particularly if repeated spells of frost and thaw have been influencing the lawn for some time. Using a 50-100 kg roller you can thus prevent grasses with roots damaged by such rising and falling of the soil surface from drying out.

It also levels the surface of the soil and increases its capillary elevation so that the moisture from deeper soil layers can reach the grass roots more easily. Heavy clayey soils should not be rolled when very wet, but only when slightly damp.

Scarification

This means mechanical "combing" of lawn growths with a set of vertically mounted steel blades of a powered or hand-driven scarifying machine. This special "rake" removes

A lawn roller fitted with steel spikes that aerate the layer of top soil.

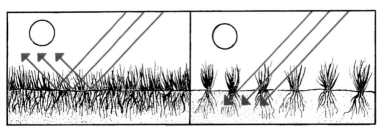

Grass growth before and after scarification.

the felt-like thin layer of tiny parts of cut grass leaves gathered close to the surface of the soil together with moss. At the same time, the surface of the soil is slightly aerated by this action. Vertical cutting of grass shoots promotes leaf growth, and the lawn is thus generally rejuvenated. Scarification also impairs and limits the growth of lawn weeds with leaf rosettes spread close to the soil. This work is usually done after mowing at the time of fullgrass growth, either in early spring or in late summer (it is usually not necessary to repeat this every year). When you finish the scarifying and remove the waste, you can fertilise and water the lawn if need be. You can also apply weedkillers or sow some grass seed on any bare patches in the lawn.

A special type of steel scarifying rake with lateral wheels that facilitate the work.

Aerating

Aerating the lawn is another useful operation, particularly beneficial for recreational lawns with much traffic. It consists in piercing or cutting the soil down to a depth of about 8 cm with the help of special tools such as rollers fitted with sharp steel spikes, blades or punches.

One of the preconditions of good lawn growth is that the layer of top soil, in which most grasses take root, should contain 10-15 per cent air. The roots need this to be able to breathe, and the underground growth nodes need it for the production of new rhizomes. If the soil surface is heavily trampled, it gets too much compacted, loses its porosity, and through this also its ideal soil air content. Through aeration, air is allowed to get into the soil, the decomposition of organic remnants is sped up, and even water and fertiliser solutions have better access to the roots. In addition, the warming up of the layer of top soil is improved, grasses can send their roots deeper into the soil and the lawn gets denser.

Aerating should be carried out at the same time as scarification. Lawns on rather heavy, clayey soils or those that are much used should be aerated twice a year: in spring (April to May), and then again in late summer (August to September).

Holes made when aerating are preferably filled with light sandy soil.

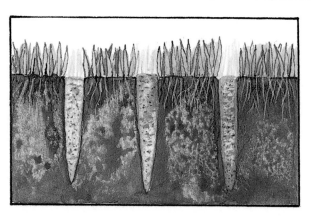

When using a fork for aerating, you may pierce the soil to a sufficient depth, but the soil around the hole is compacted even more (left). The special punching fork cuts out thin cylinders of soil, improving air access (centre). A roller equipped with sharp steel spikes does not pierce the soil sufficiently deep (right).

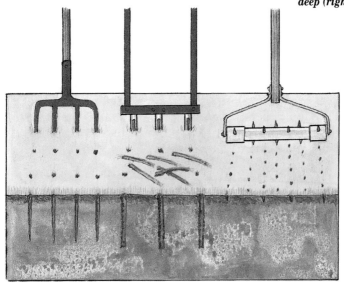

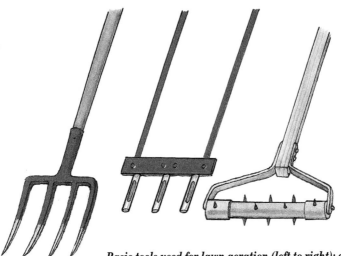

Basic tools used for lawn aeration (left to right): a steel fork, a punching fork, and a small roller with steel spikes.

Edging and surface improvement

In lawn maintenance, these jobs are recommendable but not essential. They are of a cosmetic nature: they help to perfect the appearance of your lawn. For that reason, they are mainly carried out on ornamental, representative lawns where the aesthetics play an important role - where you want to have a clear border between the lawn and a path, flowerbed or any other garden feature.

Edging

A lawn bordering on a flowerbed or a sand path usually contains some runner-forming grass species that will tend to spread into the bed as well as into the path, some species more than others. If you don't start acting immediately or don't repeat this regularly, you may find after some time that both the bed and the path are completely covered with grass.

Basic tools used for trimming lawn edges along paths or garden beds (left to right): a semicircular spade with a steel blade, a small roller with a steel cutting rosette, and steel shears with long handles.

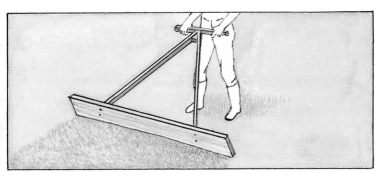

A board fitted with handles can be used for spreading the soil layer when levelling the lawn surface.

How to remove a deep hollow in the lawn (left to right): cut the turf as shown in the picture down to about 5-8 cm using a sharp spade, loosen it on both sides of the cut, fill in the hollow with good compost, replace the turf, fasten the spot with a roller and water adequately.

Surface improvement

This primarily consists of removing large or small irregularities of the terrain that may hamper mowing or water management. The three pictures above show how to proceed in levelling a deep hollow in the lawn. Smaller irregularities can be removed by spreading some soil mixed with sand, compost or humus over the newly mown lawn surface. Spreading a layer not thicker than 1.5 cm can be done

with a broom, a rake, a metal frame, a mat or some netting spread in a frame. This usually improves the overall state of the lawn. Sand renders the soil surface more porous, so water and air can penetrate more easily, it also accelerates the decomposition of organic matter that otherwise tends to form an unwanted felt-like layer. At the same time, the turf can better regenerate. This work should of course be done immediately after scarification and aerating.

Lawn diseases and pests

Almost every gardening book includes a section on plant diseases and pests. Lawns are not immune against such threats either.

Lawn diseases

These may be either contagious or non-contagious. Contagious or infectious diseases spread rapidly under favourable conditions and can attack large stretches of lawn. Non-infectious (also known as physiological) diseases are caused by unfavourable living conditions such as the soil being too dry or too wet, too acid or too alkaline, or a lack of available nutrients. If a lawn is well laid and maintained, it is usually highly resistant to diseases.

Infectious lawn diseases are mostly caused by fungi, tiny organisms lacking chlorophyll. They are unable to assimilate carbon dioxide from the air, and thus obtain their nourishment by the decomposition of their host's tissues. They are propagated by spores, by which the disease spreads to the surrounding plants. Fungal diseases, such as rusts (e.g. *Puccinia graminis*), fusarium diseases (e.g. *Fusarium nivale*), blights etc. must be combated by spraying the infested plants with a suitable fungicide, by changing conditions that are favourable to their spreading and by hardening the lawn to be more resistant against fungi. Only a specialist will probably be able to diagnose the disease properly and to find a cure - you will have to consult

Fungi that are often found forming fairy rings in grass (left to right): puffball, field agaric, Coprinus and fairy-ring toadstool.

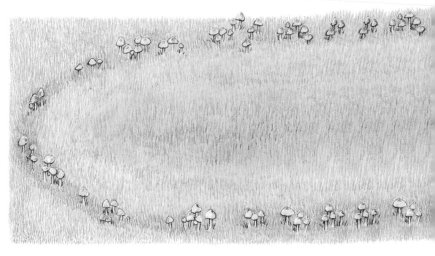

Fairy ring in grass

one if your lawn is attacked by an infection. Here, we will mention briefly only one disease, namely one caused by higher fungi, i.e. those that produce typical fruit bodies after a rainy spell. Its occurrence in the lawn is revealed by conspicuous rings in the lawn, in which the grasses grow faster at first, and then start to waste away. The fruit bodies grow along the perimeter of the so-called fairy rings, which grow wider every year and the grass is markedly darker in them. The best method to dispose of this disease is to remove the afflicted turf and the soil down to about 15 cm and replace it by new, healthy soil, which is then sown anew with an appropriate lawn mixture.

Lawn pests

Among lawn pests, we usually include various insects and their grubs, some worms and even certain vertebrates.

The **grubs** of some insect species live just below the soil surface and feed on grass roots. The afflicted grass then dies. Application of a suitable insecticide solution is a must.

Ants bite grass blades just above the soil surface. However, they usually do very little damage in garden lawns.

Earthworms are definitely no lawn pests. On the contrary, they serve as very effective aerators of the soil. On days when they crawl in greater numbers to the soil surface, they leave behind fairly large amounts of their lumpy excrements, which may be considered an aesthetic flaw.

Moles can severely damage the appearance of an intensively maintained lawn. There exists a number of "reliable" methods to get rid of them. Each of these, however, is successful only

under certain conditions and up to now there exists no general recipe for success.

Birds are dangerous to lawns immediately after sowing and when the seeds start to germinate. They often tend to peck up the seeds and tear out young plants from the soil when gathering the grubs and earthworms living in the soil. At this time lawns may be protected by nets spread over them or by placing scarecrows in their vicinity. A grown-up lawn, on the other hand, can hardly be destroyed by birds. On the contrary, they have a beneficial effect, as they destroy the grubs of various insect pests living in the turf or in the soil.

Dogs can also cause some damage. Bitches produce fairly large amounts of urine at a time, and this

Insect grubs nibbling on grass roots

A starling searching for grubs

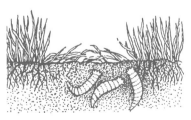

Dogs sometimes hide their "quarry" in the lawn.

has a caustic effect on the lawn, leaving rusty patches in it. Male dogs, on the contrary, use their urine to mark their territories with, and thus do very little damage to the lawn. Much more problematic both from an aesthetic and hygienic point of view are dogs' faeces on a lawn used for recreation. These should be regularly cleared away and composted or removed in some other way. Large, heavy dogs also tend to make their paths in the lawn, and some often even dig the soil.

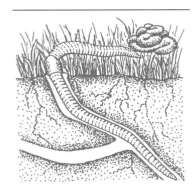

An earthworm partly hidden in its tunnel and a heap of its casts above.

A mole beside its hill

Annual ornamental grasses

As the title suggests, in this section we will discuss ornamental grasses that are grown and used in the same way as annual flowers. Their life cycle is very fast and short. They germinate in early spring, grow quickly, produce flowers in summer, and in the autumn they bear seeds and die. Among the best known annual grasses are commonly grown crops such as wheat, rye, barley, oats and maize. Annual ornamental grasses have a very similar life cycle.

Only a small number of annual ornamental grasses is grown in gardens. There are, however, quite a few wild annual species, usually neglected or described as "weeds" of our gardens and lawns. A grass that is found fairly often growing spontaneously on lawns is *Poa annua*, the fastest developing grass species. It can form three seed-producing generations during one growing season - it flowers from early spring till the first frosts. It avoids too dry as well as overly damp situations, but it tolerates both strongly acid and overfed soils. It is a ubiquitous inhabitant of heavily trampled places where all the other grass species have already died out.

In specialised literature, no more than 20 annual grass species and varieties are usually mentioned, only some five of these being grown in gardens. Lack of seed is the main reason why not more of them are used as ornamentals.

Annual ornamental grasses can be easily raised in pots in a window or in a glasshouse, and then planted in beds.

The use of annual ornamental grasses

They can be used as a component of flower beds, in which their airy elegance is a welcome feature, and their flowering stems can also be cut, dried and used for winter decoration. Inflorescences designated for drying should be cut early, before they ripen and start to decompose.

*Drying bundles of annual
ornamental grasses*

They are best tied in bundles and dried
suspended with their spikes turned
downwards in a dry, cold, airy room,
protected from direct sun.

Cultivation

Annual ornamental grasses may
be sown directly where they are to grow
after the late spring frosts, or the raised
plants can be planted there. The latter
flower earlier than the former.

*Inflorescences of some annual
ornamental grasses*

Briza maxima

Greater Quaking Grass

This genus includes only some twelve species of both annual and perennial grasses growing in Europe, Africa, Asia and South America.

Greater quaking grass is an annual grass native to the Mediterranean. It reaches a height of 40-50 cm and has rough slender leaves. It flowers from May till August. The stalk bears a sparse, unilateral smooth-stemmed panicle with up to fifteen pendent, fairly large, whitish, heart-shaped spikelets. They have a characteristic shape of flat little cones pointing downwards with their tips. Because of them it is hard to mistake this grass for any other grass species.

Detail of spike

Use

Dried inflorescences are used for room decoration in winter. For this purpose, the flowering stems are cut as soon as petal tips start to appear in the spikelets. They are bound into small bundles and dried in the shade.

Cultivation

Seeds should be sown in April directly where the grass is to grow, but raising in boxes, troughs or pots is also possible. This species likes light, but is otherwise quite undemanding.

Spikes of briza look wonderful in dried bunches.

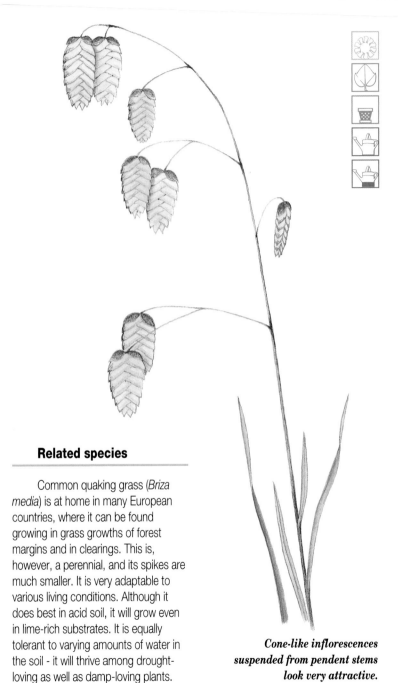

Related species

Common quaking grass (*Briza media*) is at home in many European countries, where it can be found growing in grass growths of forest margins and in clearings. This is, however, a perennial, and its spikes are much smaller. It is very adaptable to various living conditions. Although it does best in acid soil, it will grow even in lime-rich substrates. It is equally tolerant to varying amounts of water in the soil - it will thrive among drought-loving as well as damp-loving plants.

Cone-like inflorescences
suspended from pendent stems
look very attractive.

Hordeum jubatum

Foxtail Barley or Squirrel-tail Grass

This grass species reaches about 50-70 cm in height and its flowers are produced in June and July. Particularly attractive are its spikes fitted with long, fine awns that have a pinkish to purplish shade towards the tips. It can last up to three years in one place if conditions are favourable.

Use

It is grown for its ornamental character, being used as a component of cut flower arrangements. Equally interesting, however, may be a bed of this grass placed in a lawn. Fine, soft colour tones of the veil of reddish awny spikes contrast wonderfully with the green lawn, producing a pleasant, calming effect.

In older specialised literature it is particularly recommended for so-called Makart bouquets. These were freely bound bouquets of dried and prepared plants in which dried spikes of ornamental grasses played an important role, particularly those of pampas grass. These bouquets were named after the Austrian painter H. Makart (died 1884), and their origin can be placed around 1870. They were much in vogue for home decoration at that time.

Related species

Even the wild-growing wall barley (*Hordeum murinum*) has some ornamental qualities; it is also an annual plant, but it often overwinters. The spikes resemble those of barley or rye, but the plants are quite low. They are usually found growing in uncultivated soil.

Unripe spikes are an attractive complement of cut flowers in a vase.

Foxtail barley

Although barley (*Hordeum sativum*) is an agricultural crop grown for its grain, its spikes are very decorative, too, and there is no reason why we shouldn't use them in flower arrangements. The spikes with their long, tough awns have always been an important ornamental feature of harvest festival wreaths, which often used to decorate village homes until the next harvest.

Cultivation

The seeds are sown either in March in hotbeds or in pots or boxes, or in May directly in their final growing position. The spikes should be cut when they are most attractively coloured, usually during July. If left to ripen, the seeds fall out of the spikes and new plants grow spontaneously in the same spot the following year.

Lagurus ovatus

Hare's-tail Grass

This is the only representative of the genus *Lagurus*. Native to the Mediterranean, it is an annual to biennial plant ornamental mostly because of its inflorescence. It forms fairly sparse tufts of 10-50 cm tall stalks with densely hairy sheaths and leaves.

It is mostly grown for its inflorescence. The one-flowered spikelets have awl-shaped (sagittate) glumes, up to 1 cm long, densely covered from top to bottom with feathery hairs. The white hairs of the glumes cover almost the whole inflorescence, with only the jointed awns, slightly twisted in their lower parts, protruding. Flowering takes place in June and July.

Use

This is one of the most favourite annual ornamental grasses used both in flower beds and for cutting, particularly for dried winter arrangements. Even fresh, green inflorescences look attractive in flower bouquets. Its common name in many languages (hare's-tail grass) refers to the resemblance of the inflorescences to that part of a hare's body.

Cultivation

You can sow the seeds already in September in bowls covered with glass, under which the pricked-out seedlings also overwinter. In February the seedlings can be planted individually in pots and then in August they can be replanted into beds. Another possible method is to sow into a hotbed in March. This is a suitable plant for sunny, warm situations with a rather light, not very damp soil, and also for rockeries.

Lagurus ovatus always finds its place in bouquets of cut flowers. Even freshly cut inflorescences can be used.

Seeds

Spikes

*A clump of plants growing
among stones*

Setaria italica

Foxtail Millet

This is one of the large number of members of this genus, which includes about 100 species native to the warm and temperate zones of the world. Foxtail millet has been grown in Central Europe since the Bronze Age, predominantly as fodder. It attains a height of 1 m and flowers from July to September. It forms spikes densely packed in slender yellowish pseudospikes that are 1.5-3 cm thick.

Use

It was mostly grown in Europe in the Middle Ages, but its importance has been continuously waning and today it is usually only grown as food for cage birds, very occasionally also for poultry. However, the ornamental value of its pseudospikes is indisputable. It is used particularly often in dried flower arrangements. Ripe grains do not tend to fall out, so you can collect the inflorescences as late as at the time of full ripeness.

This species' spikes find their use even in small dried flower arrangements.

Cultivation

The seeds are sown in April directly in beds. Of course, raising in pots is also possible. The grains start to germinate when the soil warms up to about 8 °C. Germination is safer, however, when the soil temperature reaches about 10-15 °C. It tends to root very deep. At first its growth is relatively slow and it needs good watering, but as soon as it takes root properly, growth accelerates and the need for watering decreases.

It needs a relatively warm situation and soil. It can be used in the garden as a kind of screen to hide some less attractive places or to provide a visual separation between certain garden sections.

Part of a flowering plant with the fairly long "tail-like" spikes. The flowering stems bear leaves.

Perennial ornamental grasses

Perennial ornamental grasses have a role in the garden similar to that of all other plants grown for decoration. They can be grown for their inflorescences as well as for their leaves, or for both, and can either be planted directly among flowers to get some variety of shape, or as solitary plants to underline their specific ornamental features. Two basic types can be recognised according to their habit: tufted and stalky ones.

Tufted grasses

These have a dense ground tuft of leaves, from which slender, sparsely leaved stalks grow at the time of flowering. The individual plants need space to make the most of their shape.

A stalky grass

They will also need individual care. Each tuft has to be cleaned properly in spring, old leaves must be removed and the early-flowering species must furthermore be rid of dry stalks after flowering.

Stalky grasses

The stalky species bear most their leaves on the stalks. When in full growth, they look like green columns and can thus be grown in larger numbers, being well able to form a green wall. Their cultivation is easier than that of the tufted grasses. At the end of the growing season, even in spring with some species, they should be cut back down to the ground. At this time, however, they lack their ornamental qualities until they start to grow anew.

There are very few species in this group that might be used as a soil cover. Even with those, it is hardly possible to cover spaces larger than several square metres. They can therefore never be used as a lawn substitute.

In addition to true grasses, also some member of the genera *Carex* and *Luzula* will be mentioned in this book. Strictly botanically speaking, they belong to different families, but they bear a close resemblance to grasses and are used in gardens in the same way as grasses.

Use of perennial grasses

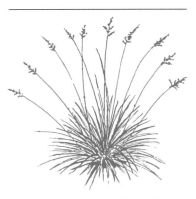

A tufted grass

Ornamental grasses are often used in gardens to create a "natural" effect, particularly near areas of water or next to a group of larger woody plants. The choice of true grasses (Gramines) for damp and strongly shaded situations, however, is very limited. On the other hand, there are many sedges (*Carex* sp.) suitable for such places.

Many grass species, by contrast, tolerate or even welcome sunny or even hot situations and very low atmospheric humidity. They can therefore easily be grown even on balconies or in portable containers in cities. They must, however, be provided with a sufficiently deep layer of soil.

A garden design with perennial grasses at the beginning of September.
*The tallest grass is **Miscanthus sinensis***

Bouteloua gracilis and *Briza media*

Mosquito Grass and Common Quaking Grass

Both two medium-tall grasses grown particularly for their interesting inflorescences.

Bouteloua gracilis

Mosquito Grass

This fine grass is native to the central regions of the United States. Originally a prairie species, it prefers sunny, rather dry situations, being particularly intolerant of winter dampness. In gardens, it is mostly grown as a rarity. The flowering season is from mid-July to mid-August, exceptionally till the end of August. The slender, erect stalks usually reach about 35 cm in height, in wet years even up to 60 cm.

The inflorescences can be used for decoration either fresh or dried. Each clump produces many stalks, but these grow in gradually. It can be grown as a solitary specimen or in small groups with drought-loving perennials planted in between. This species can be propagated by the division of clumps or from seed, but the seedlings have to be raised in pots.

Detail of inflorescence of mosquito grass

Habit of mosquito grass

Habit of common quaking grass

Inflorescence of common quaking grass

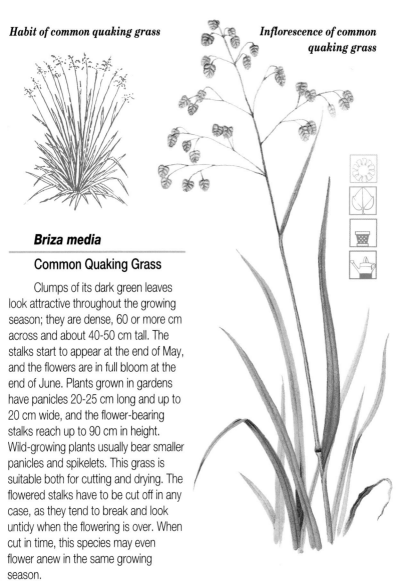

Briza media

Common Quaking Grass

Clumps of its dark green leaves look attractive throughout the growing season; they are dense, 60 or more cm across and about 40-50 cm tall. The stalks start to appear at the end of May, and the flowers are in full bloom at the end of June. Plants grown in gardens have panicles 20-25 cm long and up to 20 cm wide, and the flower-bearing stalks reach up to 90 cm in height. Wild-growing plants usually bear smaller panicles and spikelets. This grass is suitable both for cutting and drying. The flowered stalks have to be cut off in any case, as they tend to break and look untidy when the flowering is over. When cut in time, this species may even flower anew in the same growing season.

It can be recommended for gardens of an informal, natural style, particularly for heath sections. It needs rather poor, acid soils, and no fertiliser. It is propagated by the division of clumps, but also by self-seeding.

Detail of spikelet of common quaking grass

Calamagrostis
x *acutiflora*

This tall stalky reed grass is more interesting for its inflorescence than for its leaves. A cross between two species, *C. epigeios* and *C. arundinacea*, both common to damp forest places is usually grown as an ornamental. The greatest advantage of the cross is that it is not too invasive and that its stalks are firm, so that the clump does not tend to spread when older. Otherwise it does not differ from the parent species at first sight.

This grass forms slender, rigidly erect clumps the height of a grown-up man (160-180 cm). The stalks are covered with deep to dark green leaves up to halfway up. The narrowly conical panicles of spikes appear after mid-

Habit

June. They are greyish green, are fluffy in full bloom, with a marked reddish purple veil. After flowering they contract, to only about 2 cm in diameter; their reddish tint disappears and the colour turns to brownish. In the autumn, the stalks start turning yellow first, followed by the leaves only much later, at the end of October. Dry stalks together with the panicles will last long into the winter. They are used for dried arrangements.

Care of this grass is quite simple - you just have to cut the clumps back down to the earth in early spring. New shoots start to appear in April, and the growth is very fast, so that in mid-May you can have nice columns of new stalks.

It has very few demands on the soil, preferring loamy, rather acid substrates and sufficient moisture. Full sun or light shade is best. It is mostly planted in the background of flower groups among tall perennials.

Detail of spikelet

Calamagrostis x acutiflora
in full bloom

Contracted panicle after flowering

Carex sp.
Sedge

Although bearing a close resemblance to true grasses by their shape, botanically, sedges belong to a completely different order - Cyperales. Gardeners will quite easily distinguish them from grasses by the construction of the stalk. In true grasses, the stalk is usually circular in cross section, hollow, with full nodes, while in sedges it is triangular, nodeless and full inside. Most sedges grow in damp to wet places in acid soils, but this is not a rule. There also exist drought-loving species.

Flowering mountain sedge

Carex montana
Mountain Sedge

This short to medium-tall sedge is cultivated exclusively for its leaves and habit. It is a European species growing in light forests and relatively dry grassy places in sunny regions with humus-rich, alkaline soil.

In adult age it forms regular clumps, 20-30 cm tall and up to 50 cm across, with long, fine, slightly spreading leaves. These are light green at first, turning darker with age until they reach a golden brown shade in October. This coloration then lasts long into the winter.

This species is propagated by the division of clumps, but the detached parts should be raised in pots. They are then planted singly or in small groups in rockeries or in borders around woody plants. They will last over 5 years in one place.

Habit of **Carex grayi**

Carex grayi

This sedge is interesting both for its tidy habit and for its flowers and fruits. The clump reaches 70-80 cm in height. When they start to appear, they are pale green with yellowish bronze tips, in summer the colour changes to fresh green, and at the end of October they are yellowish brown. The inflorescence, and later also the infructescence, is globular in shape, consisting of pointed follicles. They can also be used for cutting.

This sedge can be planted in larger groups, and it will last in one place for quite a number of years. When in continuously wet surroundings, it will tolerate more sun. If conditions are favourable, it may even self-seed, otherwise it should be propagated by division.

Carex grayi *with flowers*

Detail of the triangular sedge stem

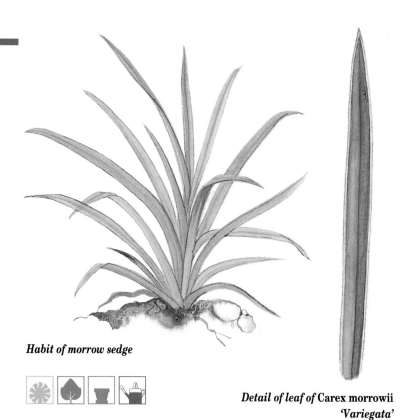

Habit of morrow sedge

Detail of leaf of Carex morrowii *'Variegata'*

Carex morrowii

Morrow Sedge

This is one of the most handsome evergreen sedges. It tends to form colonies by its slow-growing runners. Only the form 'Variegata' with dark green, narrowly pale-edged leaves is usually found in cultivation. The leaves are stiff and glossy, the new ones appearing in spring from mid-April, but they grow very slowly; not until the end of June do they cover the old ones.

A non-flowering clump reaches 40-50 cm in height. The flowers, opening at the beginning of May, are quite inconspicuous. An older colony composed of several clumps may measure over 60 cm in diameter. This species is propagated by the division of clumps carried out in spring, the detached parts must be raised in pots and then planted out with a well-formed rootball. As it is intolerant of winter sun, a shaded situation is a must, even in winter. It should also be protected from the wind, and it is better to cover it for the winter.

Carex muskingumensis *in flower*

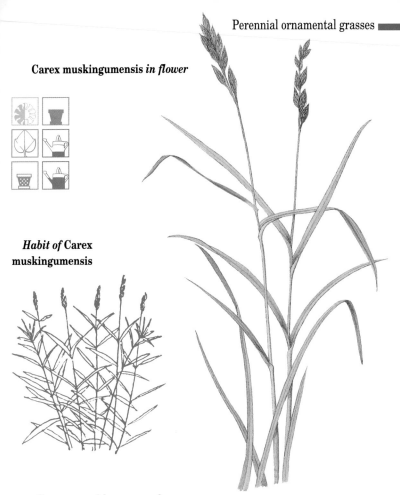

***Habit of* Carex muskingumensis**

Carex muskingumensis

This medium-size stalky sedge is particularly attractive for its dense, fine pale green leaves.

Its size in gardens varies from 70 to 90 cm in height, depending on the amount of water in the soil; its clumps may measure about 50 cm across. It is a slow spreader. It makes a good soil cover and will last for more than five years in one place. It starts to sprout in April, in the second half of May already attaining about 30 cm in height and beginning to fulfil its function. During September it turns yellowish green, and later on even a rusty colour. The flowers are produced in June. In winter the clumps should be cut back down to the earth - this is all care this species needs. It is planted in small groups close to water or in front of dark woody plants, best in light shade. If sufficiently provided with water, it will tolerate even full sun, but never really hot situations. It is easily propagated by division in spring.

Cortaderia selloana

Pampas Grass

This robust tufted grass comes from the pampas of South America. It is highly decorative, but is quite difficult to grow in the open outside the wine-growing regions.

Detail of inflorescence

Dried inflorescences look wonderful in winter arrangements.

Cultivation

It needs a sunny, warm situation and an abundance of water and nutrients in the growing season. Outside the growing season, in winter, it needs a good protection of the rootball from frost and particularly from winter dampness. It can therefore be grown with success only where good deep drainage is provided and where the growing period is sufficiently long and warm for the flowers to be formed. This is a dioecious species, and the female inflorescences are more attractive. Because of to this, you should not plant seedlings of unknown origin.

Cortaderias sprout quite late in spring and very slowly. In the summer months they are mostly attractive because of the size of the clumps. Their real beauty, however, is in their flowers, which are produced in September-October. At that time the long, strong stalks (up to 3 metres tall) bear robust white inflorescences resembling those of rushes. The inflorescences may be used for cutting and drying, but they have to be cut at the beginning of flowering, otherwise they will disintegrate.

Cortaderia selloana *'Pumila'*

Cortaderia selloana
'Sunningdale Silver'

Overwintering of cortaderias

Before the first frosts it is necessary to secure the clumps against winter; they must be protected from winter dampness and the rootballs from freezing. One possible method is to cut back the stalks and bind the leaves into a knot during dry weather. Around the clump on the ground, a plastic "collar" is spread; this should be as wide as possible to prevent rainwater from reaching the roots from the sides. The clump is then covered with straw or dry leaves. Over this protective layer, a waterproof box lined with polystyrene is turned upside down to protect the grass from frost. This protective cover should not be removed before the last frosts are over.

Propagation

Cortaderias are propagated by the division of clumps after flowering, but the detached new plants must be put in pots to take root and kept in a warm place with relatively high atmospheric humidity. You will hardly manage without a glasshouse and without some deeper knowledge; it is therefore better to get a new plant from a specialised shop or gardening firm. Planting should be carried out exclusively in spring.

Recommended varieties

'Sunningdale Silver' is over 3 metres tall and has a pure white, silky glossy, fluffy inflorescence. The clump is usually 1.5-2 m wide and the leaves are about 1 m long.

'Pumila' is an early-flowering variety, and therefore more reliable for producing flowers in our climatic conditions. The stalks are 1.5-1.8 m tall, and the leaf clumps are about 50 cm tall and wide. The inflorescence is coloured cream white. 'Rosea' has an inflorescence pinkish.

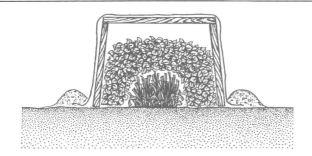

The cut-back clump prepared for overwintering is covered with dry leaves and then with a waterproof and frost-proof wooden box, which is further covered with a plastic foil that prevents water from getting to the plant.

Deschampsia caespitosa
Tufted Hair-grass

This tall tufted grass is common in damp to wet forest clearings and in light woods, in heavy, nourishing, often acid soils. It is widespread throughout the Northern Hemisphere, reaching high up towards the north and into the mountains.

It is grown in gardens for its neat appearance throughout most of the year. It sprouts very early, at the end of March or the beginning of April. At the beginning of May the tufts are already coloured fresh green, later the green turns darker. In mid-October the grass turns yellow to pale brown. The tufts should be cut back in early spring. Clumps several years old are 50-60 cm tall and over 1 m across.

Habit at the beginning of flowering

The flowering takes place in June and July. The panicles are pale golden green, turning to pale straw yellow after flowering. This species tends to self-seed profusely, so the yellowing panicles should be cut off in time.

Cultivation and use

Because of its large size, it is usually grown singly or only a few specimens together in gardens, only in parks it is used in larger groups. This is a very adaptable species; if not left without water, it will even thrive in full sun. Being quite variable, it is cultivated in several varieties differing in size, time of flowering and coloration of panicles. Varieties can be propagated exclusively by division, and they should not be left to self-seed, otherwise they will gradually disappear.

Cultivated varieties

'Bronzeschleier' is a tall variety with bronze-brown spikelets. 'Goldgehänge' is lower, spreading, with panicles coloured at first greenish gold, in full bloom attaining a striking golden

Detail of spikelet

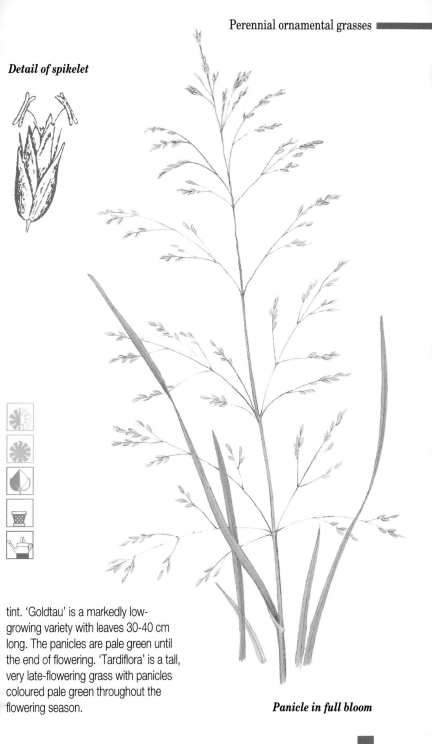

tint. 'Goldtau' is a markedly low-growing variety with leaves 30-40 cm long. The panicles are pale green until the end of flowering. 'Tardiflora' is a tall, very late-flowering grass with panicles coloured pale green throughout the flowering season.

Panicle in full bloom

Festuca sp.
Fescue

There is a large number of fescue species and subspecies, some of them very difficult to distinguish. The low-growing and tufted ones are usually grown for ornament.

Festuca glauca

Blue Fescue

This is the most beautiful and most commonly cultivated low-growing fescue. Its leaves are more greyish pruinose than those of sheep's fescue. In certain ornamental varieties that have been propagated vegetatively, the pruinose cover is so thick that it completely hides the green colour of the leaves, stalks and panicles. The stalks are thicker than those of sheep's fescue, and are, together with the panicles, rigidly erect, resembling

needles in a pincushion. It starts flowering at least a week later than sheep's fescue. The flower-bearing stalks are silvery white in colour, the panicles are silvery yellow. Some varieties have coloured stalks, exclusively in a bluish purple shade.

In the wild, it can be found growing in dry, sunny places - so it should be provided with similar conditions even in cultivation. It tends to rot in damp soils, and black spots form on the leaves during rainy summers. The tufts have to be cleaned individually in spring, and stalks cut off after

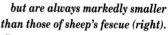

Blue fescue (right) forms dense tufts of tough, prickly leaves, which may be of various sizes and variously coloured, but are always markedly smaller than those of sheep's fescue (right).

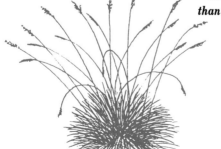

flowering to prevent self-seeding, as the seedlings might lose the beautiful silvery shade of the parent plants. These should be propagated exclusively by division, which is done in late summer. The detached plants are planted in pots in a sandy substrate, which should not be left to dry out until the plants take root. Young plants with a properly developed rootball thrive better when planted out.

The smallest varieties are suitable for rockeries, the taller ones are planted among low-growing perennials of steppe-like character. You should however always have in mind that the tufts have to be divided and replanted after 3-5 years.

Cultivated varieties

'Frühlingsblau' has fine silvery grey leaves with a marked bluish shade. The tufts are up to 20 cm tall, and in older age over 30 cm wide.

Within the species, 'Bergsilber' is a relatively robust variety. It is coloured a light silvery grey, turning bluish to greenish grey towards the autumn. The tufts are regular, semiglobular in shape, attaining over 25 cm in height and 35 cm in width in older age.

Flowering variety
'Frühlingsblau'

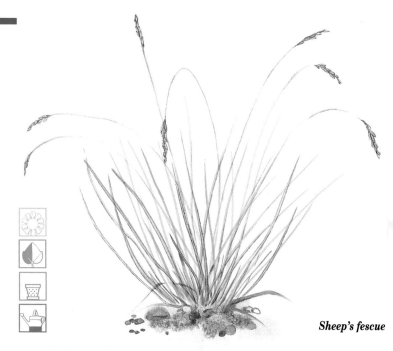

Sheep's fescue

Festuca ovina

Sheep's Fescue

This is a highly variable, densely tufted fescue with long bristle-like leaves. These are bluish to greyish pruinose, but the basic green colour always prevails. When bearing flowers, the upper parts of the stalks are conspicuously golden pink, pink to almost cyclamen, but never bluish purple. The flowering starts earlier (7-10 days) than in blue fescue, and the plants are more robust. The tufts reach 30-40 cm in height, the stalks grow knee-high. Older clumps may measure about 70 cm across, with spread stalks even up to 1 m.

In the wild, it inhabits sandy, acid, dry soils. It is quite undemanding in gardens, and if provided with conditions of its natural home, it may last over 5 years in one spot. This is a highly variable species, therefore only selected, vegetatively propagated types are used in gardens. These should not be left to self-seed, the stalks must therefore be cut off after flowering. In early spring the tufts have to be cleaned by removing the remnants of dead leaves from the previous year. This should be done by hand, each tuft individually, which may be quite laborious; you should therefore plant only small groups of 3-5 tufts. In such an arrangement their shape also stands out better.

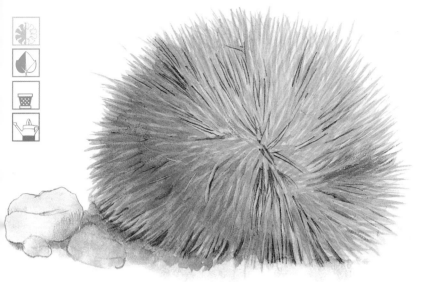

Variety 'Pic Carlit'

The variety 'Aprilgrün' forms medium-large regular tufts sprouting already in mid-April. 'Superba' is a robust fescue with globular tufts up to 45 cm tall. Both these will last about 5 years in one place, if given sufficient space. 'Solling' is a poor grower and it almost does not flower; you will thus be spared the laborious job of cleaning away the flowered stalks.

Festuca scoparia

It is better known in gardening under the name *Festuca crinum ursi*. It forms fresh green compact tufts made of tangled long, tough, bristle-like leaves which look particularly well if allowed to grow as if "running down" from a slope. If grown on flat ground, it tends to spread in an unsightly way and where two neighbouring tufts meet, they rise into dishevelled waves. The flowers are inconspicuous and rather a disturbing element than an ornament. The tuft is 15-20 cm tall, increasing very fast in width; within 2-3 years after planting it may be about 30 cm across.

This fescue is an ideal feature for large rockeries or for covering the soil among dwarf conifers on sloping terrain. It does not have to be mown nor cleaned in spring. It can last several years in a suitable, slightly shaded, not very warm place. If the situation is too sunny and dry, the tufts start to dry out from the centre after 4-5 years.

The favourite variety 'Pic Carlit' grows much slower. Instead of flat tufts, it forms neat dense cushions that retain their green colour through winter almost till the next spring. The leaves are shorter than in the species, tough, prickly. It is particularly suitable for rockeries.

Helictotrichon sempervirens

Blue Oat Grass

This tall tufty plant with graceful leaves and flowers is one of the most important ornamental grasses.

The leaves are slender, tough, pointed, and markedly greenish grey to silvery blue. The tufts are regular, dense, semiglobular, about 60 cm tall and slightly more in width. Flowering takes place in June. The stalks, 150 cm tall, are flexible, almost leafless, spreading into a wide fan, slightly bending. The golden panicles, spread when in full bloom, are contracted later on along the stalk. They ripen and turn dry fairly rapidly. Then they should be cut off as deep among the leaves as possible. This is quite laborious, but the tuft of silvery leaves is then a true gem until late autumn. It remains green almost continuously, but the beauty of the leaves may be spoiled in damp winters. This is why the old leaves should be removed in early spring by cutting them off or better still by combing them out. The new leaves sprout early - at the beginning of April - and they can start playing their ornamental role again from mid-May.

Cultivation and use

It is propagated by division, but the detached parts have to be raised in

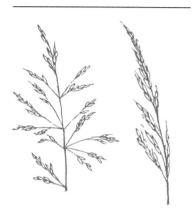

Panicle in full bloom (left) and after flowering

Habit

pots. Because of its large size, beautiful habit, but also because of the rather laborious cleaning, it is usually planted singly or in small groups of 3-5 plants with sufficiently large spaces in between (about 80 cm). It needs sunny, rather dry situations, and there it may last for some five years or more. It does not live so long where the soil is damp and heavy.

Blue oat grass

Luzula sylvatica
Great Wood Rush

Botanically, members of the genus *Luzula* are much closer to liliaceous plants than to true grasses. This is best revealed if you inspect their flowers under a magnifying glass. As far as their habit and, particularly, their leaves are concerned, they greatly resemble grasses.

Great wood rush is a low-growing, tufty plant forming a number of runners, by which it spreads to form carpets covering an area of several square metres. It is common in damp mountain forests in acid soils.

Its leaves are over 1 cm wide, finely grooved, hairy on the underside, coloured grass green. They are arranged in funnel-shaped rosettes of various sizes. The plants form dense, but rather untidy carpets. A single plant is able to produce a colony measuring 50 cm across in 3-4 years. Its flowers appear in April-May; they are tiny, dark brown, and arranged in wide-branching cymes borne on 30-40 cm tall stalks.

Cultivation and care

It should be protected from winter sunshine (it is usually covered with snow in its natural habitat) and from drought, otherwise the leaf tips start to turn dry and look unsightly until late spring of the next year, when newly sprouted leaves cover them. Flowers should be removed after flowering.

This species is mostly used for covering the soil among evergreen woody plants in damp, peaty soils.

It is not greatly bothered by the presence of the roots of grown-up trees. It can be combined with various taller ferns, but low-growing, tiny ferns and shade-loving perennials, however, might be stiffled by it. Individual varieties differ only slightly, mostly in the width of their leaves and their ability to spread. 'Marginata' is an interesting variety with leaves bordered by a sharply defined, narrow, whitish yellow margin.

Detail of flower

*A flowering specimen producing
a daughter plant*

Melica sp.

Melic

Members of the genus *Melica* only started to be grown when garden styles imitating nature became popular. So far, they are still not much cultivated. Two European species are commonly used in gardens.

Melica ciliata
Silky-spike Melic

This is a medium-tall, tuft-forming grass native to warm and relatively dry parts of Europe, but not to the Mediterranean. It is usually found in sunny, stony situations. It is very neat-looking and is particularly suitable for dry sections of gardens - not only natural-look ones, but those of classic design as well. The leaf tufts are about 40 cm tall, dense, fine-structured, coloured a fairly pale shade of greyish green. It flowers from the end of May to July. The cylindrical spikes are pale brown, whitish when ripe. They are borne on slender stalks arranged in an erect fan and last until the second half of summer. Then they should be removed. The flowering tufts are 60-70 cm tall and 70-100 cm wide when the flowered stalks start to spread. This species is not particularly interesting after flowering, but it retains its green colour until mid-September. It is easily propagated from seed, but division, carried out in spring, is also possible.

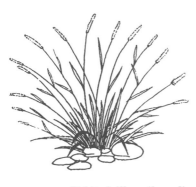

Habit of silky-spike melic

Melica transsilvanica
Transylvanian Melic

It is taller than the former species, the tufts reaching a height of 60-70 cm, over 80 cm when in flower, but they are more sparse. The cylindrical spikes are brownish red at first and brownish to grey later, but never greyish white as in the above species. It flowers slightly later and the stalks are more bent. Propagation is easy, from seed.

It is suitable for steppe-like garden sections which should have a natural look, not for formal arrangements.

**Silky-spike
melic**

Miscanthus sp.

Silver Grass or Sword Grass

These robust stalky grasses native to East Asia are grown for their stately appearance. They are rather reminiscent of rushes, but because of their size they can even be likened to bamboos. Being totally hardy, they can be used as a substitute for the delicate bamboos in harsher climatic conditions. However, they are not an evergreen.

Miscanthus floridulus

This is the most robust of the miscanthuses, reaching up to 3 m in height, and is most commonly used in the place of bamboos, but it has a rather more unwieldy, less sophisticated appearance. It sprouts late, not before early May, but then it grows quickly. It is knee-high within a month, by the end of June reaching a man's height. Until mid-October it then adorns the garden, forming green columns or screens. Then it turns yellow to ochre and remains standing stiff throughout the winter. It should be cut back in spring, immediately before sprouting, never in the autumn. The stalks are woody, the same as bamboo canes, and can be used in a similar way.

Miscanthus floridulus produces flowers only rarely, and these are not particularly attractive.

Miscanthus floridulus is an undemanding species, but it produces a large amount of growth every year, so it needs a soil rich in nutrients. It prefers damp conditions in summer and autumn, but it will tolerate even drought, light shade and the presence of roots of surrounding trees; it can thrive for many years in such places. If given sufficient space, five-year-old tufts may measure more than a metre above the soil, being naturally wider at the top.

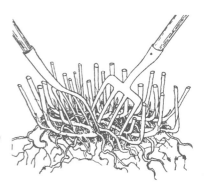

It can be easily propagated by the division of clumps before sprouting, but you will need some strength and good tools (preferably a good fork and sharp secateurs).

Miscanthus floridulus

Miscanthus sinensis 'Strictus'

Miscanthus sinensis

Its height and time of flowering vary greatly, but even the most lush-growing types never reach the size of *Miscanthus floridulus*.

Early varieties which already start flowering at the end of August and the beginning of September are grown mostly for their flowers. The inflorescences have the form of large shaggy tassels coloured in youth from silvery pinkish to a brownish red flesh colour, depending on the variety. When the flowering is over, all these tassels turn silvery grey, but never silvery white.

Late varieties flower only exceptionally, being grown primarily for their interesting leaves which have

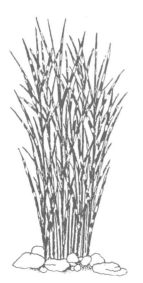

Habit of **Miscanthus sinensis 'Strictus'**

Habit of **Miscanthus sinensis 'Silberfeder'**

misscanthus sinensis
(stricthus)
L.d.l oct 2001

Miscanthus sinensis
'Gracillimus'

...ey are used in flower
...nts, both fresh and dried. It is
...wn singly, forming green
...50-170 cm tall and 70-90 cm

...tus', commonly known as
...rass, has leaves with
...lowish white stripes. They
...lant with only their tips
...ihtly bending. It reaches
...September, the tassels are over 20 cm ...100-150 cm ...in height and the tufts are
long, very pale-coloured, silvery, with 75-80 cm across. It is very late-
a pinkish to lilac shade when young. flowering, producing flowers only rarely.

'Graziella', also early-flowering, 'Variegatus' has longitudinally
has tufts of fine leaves 80-100 cm tall white-striped leaves. It is a graceful
and slender, up to 170 cm tall stalks grass, but is more tender than all the
with inflorescences coloured a flesh-like other mentioned varieties. It needs
red at first, and silvery grey later on. plenty of warmth. Its height is

'Gracillimus' is a late-flowering 160-180 cm, older tufts attain about
variety grown for its elegant, fine leaves. 100 cm in width. It practically never
These are strikingly narrow, arched in flowers.

Molinia caerulea

Purple Moor Grass

It has medium-long leaves and fairly tall flowering stalks. It starts to be attractive in the second half of summer and is particularly beautiful in its autumn coloration.

Its tough, narrow, dark green leaves form fairly short prickly tufts. It starts sprouting as late as the first half of May and is a slow grower, so its tufts are quite shapely but fairly inconspicuous in the first half of its growing season. During August, long, tough stalks appear; these are arranged in a fan and are seemingly nodeless (in fact, the nodes are only at the base of the stalks, among the leaves). They bear narrow, compact panicles composed of tiny spikelets. In the autumn, the stalks are wonderfully coloured in various shades of yellow to orange.

Molinia caerulea ssp. *altissima* is generally more robust than the species. Flowering takes place in mid-summer, but it is most ornamental in the autumn.

Cultivation and use

Selected types propagated exclusively by division, which should be done in spring, are grown in gardens. Plants grown from seed are highly variable, and therefore not suitable for cultivation. They are grown singly or in small groups; their autumn coloration is particularly wonderful against a dark background. They are suitable for dry winter arrangements.

Cultivated varieties

Molinia caerulea 'Variegata' has yellowish white longitudinal stripes on the leaves and the inflorescence is

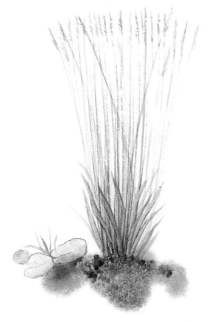

Variety 'Moorhexe' in its autumn coloration

Variety 'Heidebraut'
in its autumn
coloration

yellowish green. The whole plant makes
a very light impression. The leaves are
30-40 cm tall, the flower-bearing stalks
measure 70-80 cm.

'Moorhexe', on the contrary, is
very dark green in colour, and the stiffly
erect stalks bear black-green, narrowly
compact spikelets. The stalks turn
yellow, orange to a rusty red in autumn.
It is slightly taller than 'Variegata' but the

tufts are more slender and compact
when in flower.

'Heidebraut' is conspicuously
taller, with stalks arranged in a wide fan.
The spikelets are green to pale
brownish when in flower, in October the
stalks turn golden yellow to orange and
the spikelets attain a rusty shade. The
leaves measure 60-80 cm, flowering
stalks are up to 140 cm tall.

Panicum virgatum

Switch Grass

This is a tall, stalky grass, ornamental by its habit, flowers, as well as its autumn coloration. It is native to North America.

Habit of a flowering specimen of variety 'Strictum'

It has densely leafy stalks, 130-150 cm tall, and reaching up to 180 cm when in flower. The plants start to sprout as late as the second half of May. By August, it forms columnar tufts with flat leaves reminiscent of those of corn. Flowering takes place from mid-August. The panicles are wide-spread, large, airy, composed of numerous tiny bead-like spikelets.

Cultivation and use

Only vegetatively propagated varieties are suitable for garden cultivation. Plants grown from seed are very variable, and therefore not safe for ornamental purposes. Switch grass is particularly attractive when planted in small groups, but it needs a good deal of space. It also needs plenty of nutrients for satisfactory growth. A sunny situation is a must; it tolerates an occasional drought an will stay in one place for many years. It can be planted singly or in small groups, combined with other, low-growing perennials or put in front of conifers.

Stalks with inflorescences can be used in a vase in their fresh state and also in dried arrangements, but it does not retain its winter coloration.

Detail of inflorescence

Recommended varieties

'Strictum' is a robust grass the stalks of which do not tend to spread during the growing season as the species does, but remain rigidly erect until winter. It is green in the growing season and yellowish orange from October.

'Rehbraun' is rather shorter than the former. Individual red-coloured leaves start appearing already during August; the autumn coloration is more intense, appearing as early as September.

'Rotstrahlbush' ('Hänse Herms') is a much poorer flowerer than the two varieties previously mentioned (80 cm in height, 120 cm when in flower), but half of its leaves attain their red colour already in August. The autumn coloration is the most intense, with reddish bronze shades prevailing.

Sesleria sp.

Moor Grass

Particularly the early-flowering species are commonly grown: *Sesleria albicans* and *Sesleria sadlerana* from Central and Western Europe and *S. heuffleriana* from the Balkans.

Sesleria sadlerana

Sesleria albicans (syn. *S. caerulea* ssp. *calcarea*) is a short tufty grass producing, as early as April, its flowering stalks bearing, cylindrical spikes with a marked bluish coloration. The tufts spread continuously, forming small colonies on rock ledges.

More commonly cultivated are the more colourful and more robust but closely related Balkan species - *Sesleria*

Habit of **Sesleria sadlerana**

Habit of **Sesleria albicans**

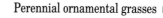

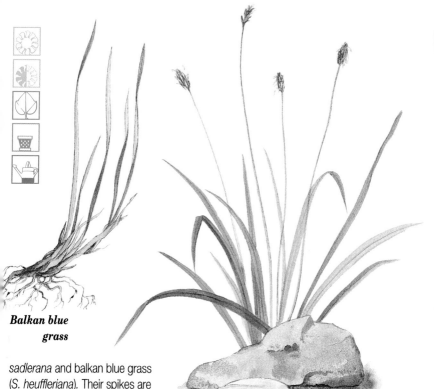

Balkan blue grass

Sesleria albicans

sadlerana and balkan blue grass (*S. heuffleriana*). Their spikes are markedly dark, of a bluish purple colour, 2-3 cm long. The leaves are greyish white pruinose on the inner side and glossy fresh green outside, so that the tufts are conspicuously bicoloured. Flowers are produced in April; as in the preceding species, the spikes appear close above the leaves at first, with the stalks gradually growing taller, until they reach their final height and start to lean out of the tuft. They should be removed at the beginning of summer, so as not to spoil the fresh green colour of the tuft. The tufts reach 40-50 cm in height, in the taller *S. heuffleriana* even over 80 cm. Both species change their colour to dark yellow or even rusty in October.

Cultivation and use

All seslerias must be cleaned in early spring, as they sprout very early and grow fast, being at their most ornamental at that time. *Sesleria albicans* and *S. sadlerana* are highly suitable for sunny rocky places, *S. heuffleriana* being more suitable for slightly shaded, not very dry situations. Propagation is by division.

Bamboos

Within the large family *Poaceae*, it is only the subfamily *Bambuseae* that includes woody plants. This subfamily comprises some 45 genera with about 500-600 species native to the tropics and subtropics, with only a few growing in the temperate zone.

Thanks to the richly branched system of rhizomes, most bamboos tend to form dense growth very rapidly. Low-growing species have stalks up to 3 m tall, those of medium-tall species reach a height of 8-12 m, and the tall species can measure 20-30 m, or even up to 60 m. The leaves are annual, but they may last for several years. Most species flower quite exceptionally, some of them once every 60-120 years, and the whole plant dies after flowering (e.g. some members of the genus *Bambusa*). Only a few species produce flowers every year and the plants do not die afterwards (e.g. species of the genera *Sasa* and *Pseudosasa*). New stalks grow either in the autumn (genus *Fargesia*) or in spring (all the other genera mentioned here).

It can generally be said that bamboos are very fast growers. At the time of their maximum growth the daily accrual may be 70-80 cm, and the stalks reach their final length within several weeks. Then the stalk stops growing in length, only forming lateral branches with leaves.

Cultivation

To grow successfully, bamboos

The high-quality wood of bamboos can be used in a number of ways.

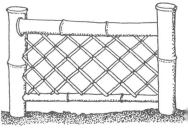

Detail of jointed bamboo stalks

need a warm, moist climate and
a sufficiently moist, light, nutrient-rich
soil. This applies most of all to the tall
species. They are intolerant of very acid
substrates. Tropical species are not
frost-resistant, while those originating
in subtropical and temperate regions
tolerate drops in temperature down
to -15 or -20 °C.

Bamboos can be propagated by
detaching the runners with a new stalk
and a rootball, or by rhizome cuttings.
In the genus *Bambusa,* it is even
possible to propagate by stem cuttings.

Being highly decorative plants,
bamboos can embellish any garden.
Some 25 species and cultivars are
grown in European gardens and parks.
They usually don't reach the same
height as in their natural surroundings,
but thanks to their grace and their
decorative character, they are
a wonderful sight all the same.

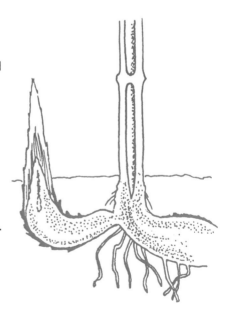

Formation of a scion

Fargesia nitida

This species is also known under the name of *Sinarundinaria nitida.* It is native to the Chinese provinces Szechwan and Khan-su. Together with *F. murialae*, this is the only representative of the so-called tufted bamboos.

A bamboo planted in a container

Its stalks usually have a purplish shade, they reach a height of up to 2 m and are at least 2 cm across at the base. The leaves are bright green above and mat below. Several stalks in each tuft reach their maximum height every year, and in the following years they produce five lateral branches from each node. Older stalks are blackish brown.

Fargesia nitida, "the umbrella bamboo", really evokes an umbrella in the way the lateral branches are attached to the main stalk. It is one of the most commonly cultivated bamboos native to the warm regions of the temperate zone. It is the hardiest of all bamboo species, and will endure our winters without any damage. Only the leaves coil in frosty weather. It is noted for its dense foliage that lasts for years.

Use

Because of its unchanging size, it is often grown singly, e.g. at the margin of a pond, or even in a container. Because of its attractiveness and positive features, it has been grown in England and in Western and Southern European countries for a century, and for a slightly shorter period in North America.

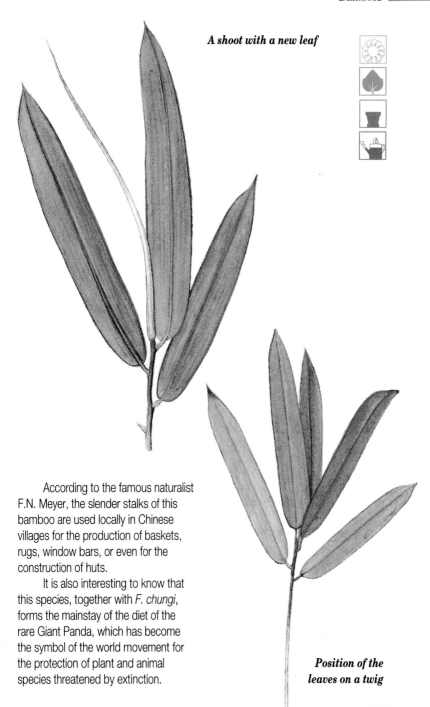

A shoot with a new leaf

According to the famous naturalist F.N. Meyer, the slender stalks of this bamboo are used locally in Chinese villages for the production of baskets, rugs, window bars, or even for the construction of huts.

It is also interesting to know that this species, together with *F. chungi*, forms the mainstay of the diet of the rare Giant Panda, which has become the symbol of the world movement for the protection of plant and animal species threatened by extinction.

Position of the leaves on a twig

115

Phyllostachys humilis

Out of some 36 species belonging to this genus, about twelve are grown in cultivation. The stalks reach 18-20 m in height, they are cylindrical in cross-section, smooth or grooved, with prominent nodes and yellow in colour. Usually two, rarely even three twigs branch from each node in the upper parts of the stalks. Young stalks appear in spring.

This species is native to Japan. It reaches 3-5 metres in height and belongs to the lowest members of the genus. It has elegant stalks, slightly pendent in their upper half. They are covered with dark green leaves. Very few lateral twigs are formed, these being markedly long. The leaves are longish lanceolate, dark green above and mat below, with 6, 8 or 10 lateral veins. They are 5-12.5 cm long and 1.5. cm wide. The leaf sheaths are faintly reddish at first. This species is often mistaken for ground bamboo, *Pleioblastus pumilus*, but it lacks the waxy cover that can be found on the stalks under the nodes of the latter.

Cultivation

It is sufficiently hardy in European winters, tolerating frosts below -20 °C or -25 °C. It is propagated by detaching the young stalks with a part of the rhizome; new plants are left to take root in a container.

A member of the genus Phyllostachys *looks very decorative in arrangements with larger stones and some small trimmed broad-leaved shrubs.*

Use

This is a very ornamental species best suitable for parks, but also for small gardens, balconies and other places where plants in containers are placed for ornament.

The typical sparse habit of this species.

Garden water feeder made of thick bamboo stalks.

Pleioblastus pumilus

Ground Bamboo

This species, sometimes also sold under the names of *P. chino* var. *viridis* f. *pumilus* or *Sasa pumila*, comes from north and central Japan. It measures 0.8 m at the most, but if grown in dry places, it is usually much lower, almost stunted. Its stalks are circular in cross-section and have a fine purplish shade. There are waxy covers under the nodes, and many lateral branches are formed in the upper parts of the stalks. The leaves are dark green, lanceolate in outline, about 9-10 cm long and 1-1.5 cm wide.

Cultivation and use

This is a commonly cultivated species in the warm parts of Western Europe, the Mediterranean and North America. It is very hardy, tolerating temperatures down to -23 °C without any damage. It likes to be partly shaded, then its ornamental leaves develop fully. When grown in full sun, it remains smaller. Being fairly undemanding and able to grow in the

Ground bamboo used as an undergrowth plant in a Japanese garden.

Position of the leaves and the typical habit of ground bamboo

vicinity of or as an undergrowth of tall trees and being a fast spreader, it is suitable for a speedy covering of large stretches of soil by greenery. The only disadvantage are the individual wide-spreading rhizomes that have to be removed. It is also a good plant for containers. It is easily propagated by detaching the rhizomes, which can be first planted and left to take root in pots.

Pleioblastus variegatus *is a similar species. It is an evergreen, of the same height, but it has white-striped leaves and spreads very slowly.*

Pseudosasa japonica

Stalks of this species are usually 2-3 metres tall, and about 2 cm across at the base. The semi-erect branches appear sparsely on the upper parts of the stalks, bearing at their ends 5-6, sometimes even up to 12, leaves. These are lanceolate, tapering into a point at the end, 20-25 cm long and 3-4 cm wide. They are glossy dark green above and faintly bluish below.

Cultivation

This is a relatively hardy oriental bamboo. It is abundant in Japan and in central Korea, but its origin is rather uncertain. It is often one of the most commonly grown bamboos in the gardens and parks of the Mediterranean, Western Europe (it has been cultivated here for over 100 years), the United States and Japan.

Top parts of a plant

Detail of the leaves, their position and shape

Habit

temperatures. In the temperate regions where there is a danger of short spells of very low temperatures, it is better to grow this species in containers or as a house plant. It may be partly damaged by frost if grown outside, but it will easily regenerate in spring. A cover of conifer loppings and dry leaves is therefore a good idea. It is propagated by detaching strong runners and planting them in pots to take root.

Use

It will form a thick growth at a rather slower pace than other runner-forming bamboos. It thrives in light to loamy soils, tolerating temperatures down to -25 °C. It is usually evergreen, particularly when the temperature does not drop below -12 °C in winter. The leaves can be damaged at lower

For its ornamental leaves and generally attractive appearance, it is an important plant for gardens and parks, particularly near water. It is also planted in cemeteries. The supple, sufficiently long-lasting stalks are used in the production of baskets and mats.

Sasa tesselata

The genus *Sasa* includes lower-growing bamboos with erect, cylindrical stalks reaching a height of about 3 metres and a width of about 1 cm at the base. There is usually only one twig growing from each node, but there may be even two. It is one of the hardiest bamboos. Some 70 species are known to grow mostly in East and Central Asia.

Sasa tesselata (also known as *Indocalamus tesselatus* or *Arundinaria tesselata*) is a large-leaved bamboo reaching heights of 1.5-2 metres. The stalk is circular in cross-section in its lower part, but slightly flattened higher up; the individual joints are 3-9 cm long.

The leaf sheaths firmly clasp the stalk, but those at the top are slightly more loose, so that the stalk seems to be thicker in its upper part. Twigs grow singly from the nodes. The large, 30-40 cm long and 6-8 cm wide leaves are quite striking. They are longish

Bamboo stalks used as a garden fence

The foliage

lanceolate, glossy dark green above and bluish below, with finely serrate margins.

Cultivation and use

This wonderful bamboo, one of the most frost-resistant, is native to China. It is commonly cultivated in the Mediterranean, in Western Europe and the warm parts of North America, in parks but particularly in gardens. It spreads rapidly after planting and is capable of forming dense growths with pendent foliage that completely hides the soil. In parks, it is usually grown in groups in damp places or along areas of water, in marginal plantings or in belts around groups of tall woody plants. It does well in shady places in gardens. This is also suitable for container greenery.

It should be propagated by carefully detaching individual runners with rootballs before new growth in spring. Rhizomes with a new stalk but without roots usually die when separated.

Shibataea kumasasa

Ruscus Bamboo

The genus *Shibataea* includes 5 species native to China and one of Japanese origin - this is the one illustrated here.

Shibataea kumasasa (synonyms *S. kamsasa, Phyllostachys kumasaca, Bambusa ruscifolia* and *B. viminalis*) has stalks that are 60-80 cm tall, ascending, relatively tough, semicircular or triangular in cross-section, with short joints less than 5 cm long. The leaves are ovoid lanceolate with pointed tips, 8-10 cm long and 2-2.5 cm wide. They are dark green in colour, smooth above, with dentate margins. The leaf sheaths are membranous, purplish at first, the same length as the stalk joints or even longer. The species is easily recognisable by the leaves, which markedly resemble those of the genus *Ruscus* (family *Liliaceae*).Hence also its English name.

Cultivation and use

It needs a damp, but not quite wet situation. Frost damage can occur when the temperatures drop below -23 ˚C. The leaves usually suffer the worst damage, but they are replaced by new ones in spring.

This unique, very ornamental bamboo species differs markedly in its appearance from all the other ones cultivated in temperate regions. It is also excellent as an undergrowth plant.

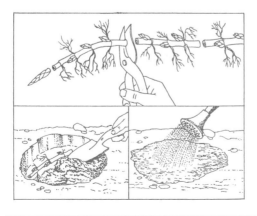

Bamboo propagation. Part of the rhizome (about 20 cm) is cut off, put in a hole made in the soil, covered with earth and watered.

Ruscus bamboo

Thanks to the shape of its leaves, *Shibataea kumasasa* can be easily distinguished from some other species, the foliage of which is reminiscent of some willows.

By way of conclusion

All bamboo species chosen for this book are to a great extent resistant to the frosty winters not uncommon in Central and Western Europe.

Bamboos have become quite fashionable at the end of this century,

both for outdoor and indoor decoration. The history of cultivation of ornamental plants shows us that a large number of species were much in vogue for some time, only to be forgotten again, and only the best species and varieties have remained to become the "fixed stars" among cultivated plants. It remains to be seen whether the bamboos offered today by many gardening firms of Western and Southern Europe will stand the test of time.

Index

Index of Scientific Names

General Index

Index

Index of Common Names